practical pointers

for TRAINING YOUR CHILD

by Lloy A. Kniss

CHRISTIAN LIGHT PUBLICATIONS, INC.
Harrisonburg, Virginia 22801

Copyright © 1975
Christian Light Publications, Inc.

First Printing 5,500
Second Printing 3,000

ISBN 0-87813-509-X

Printed in U.S.A.

FOREWORD

Someone has observed that the rearing of a family requires such resources of strength that God has wisely given it into the hands of parents in their younger and more vigorous years. Some parents, however, have felt that their task requires such resources of wisdom that only by the time their children have been brought into maturity have they actually acquired the knowledge in part necessary for the responsibilities of parenthood. Fortunately, we have in a book like this the distillation of a lifetime of practical experiences in family life. The inspiration gained by reading it will add strength for the parental task, and the wisdom to be gleaned from it will prove to be invaluable.

Lloy and Elizabeth Kniss are the parents of three sons and a daughter. This family's early experience in Christian living was wrought out on the mission field in India, in itself a tribute to both parents and children. Brother Kniss further speaks from the standpoint of a teacher, minister, and bishop in the church — work which has evidently led him into breadth of observation concerning the nature of home life and its fundamental importance to the church.

An attractive and unique feature of this book is that each chapter is introduced with a human interest story or illustration, many of which were gleaned from the experience of its author. These lead naturally into the main discussions of the respective chapters, each of which are filled with keen insight into the nature of the task of ordering the Christian home.

It gives me pleasure to commend this book to parents and to others interested in children, with the prayer that it may find wide use in undergirding our homes.

J. Ward Shank

PREFACE

"Lo, children are an heritage of the Lord: and the fruit of the womb is his reward" (Psalm 127:3).

The Lord has given me a strong love for children and young people. I believe that if we live as God has planned for us, we will find every succeeding stage of life better than the one before. I do not think it is good for us older people to look back and wish we were young again. As I look back over my seventy-five years, I remember many things I could have done better had I been a little wiser, but wishing I could do them over would be futile. I derive great pleasure in watching children and young people developing and growing. I see many who are doing much better than I did, and this gives me pleasure.

I have observed a few things in life, and I think I have learned some things. Many of the things I learned, I learned by my failures. Others I learned by observing others.

A few times in past years I have been asked to speak in public meetings about child training. Some young parents suggested that I write some of the things I said so they could read them. This is one thing that prompted this writing.

There are at least two other reasons why I decided to undertake this work. Many young parents have had little or no formal training in child training so some straight-forward, matter-of-fact suggestions might be helpful and practical. Many do not have the time to wade through a large book of involved language on the subject. There should be something brief as well as practical, from which to get the help needed.

The second reason is that many families who have had the formal training in child study or pedagogy feel they have failed with their children as they tried to train them "by the book." This may be true because some books contain unscriptural or impractical theories. These pointers

4

for child training have been made on the basis of Biblical principles, and personal intuition, observation, reason, and experience.

I trust that in training your child, you have one over-riding aim in all you do for him, and that is to help him become a child of God. We, as Christian parents, are not trying to make politicians, national patriots, movie stars, or presidents; neither are we primarily trying to make business men and women out of our children, but we first of all want them to be true Christians.

The central objective of a Christian parent is to lead his child to desire the new birth, and fit him to live victoriously.

Teaching Christian virtues and ideals to young children will not confuse them as to their need for regeneration when they come to the age of accountability. It will rather help youths to discover their inability to really live true to the virtues and ideals they have learned. How would they know sin if there had been no law? How would they feel their need of a Saviour if they had not been taught the virtues?

Love for our children does not make it easier to punish them when they need it. Only when punishing a child becomes a painful ordeal for a parent is the punishment truly effective.

In early colonial days a certain father gave his young son the ultimatum that if he repeated a certain misdeed, he would have to sleep in the loft of their log cabin. This was something the boy dreaded very much. The day came when the deed was repeated, and at bedtime, the father gave the boy a pillow and a blanket and told him to climb the ladder to the loft. The father and mother went to bed in their comfortable bedroom on the main floor. But the father couldn't sleep until he took his pillow and climbed the ladder to join his son in the loft. This is an example of effective punishment by a loving father.

Administering punishment is not the principal part of child training. But because of the modern distorted view that many have of the validity of corporal punishment, we do well to ponder its benefits as Solomon did in Proverbs.

I hope this writing will do at least two things for young parents. I trust that it will be of help in child rearing and that it might stimulate some parents to read good books on the subject of child training or child study. There are some good books available, but this does not lessen the need for us to use the principles given in God's Word.

With this writing goes my prayer for all young parents to properly train those precious jewels God has entrusted to their care.

Certainly God made no mistake when he created us so that young people would bear children and rear them, but they may at times wish they had more experience or wisdom to do what God wants them to do. May I venture the proposal that God wants older ones who have gone through that period to help the younger ones when possible? In this spirit I offer these suggestions, but do not want to impose them on anyone. I know, of course, that my knowledge is also incomplete.

The various chapters in this book are not written in sequential order, as each one is a separate article and not directly related to any other. However, the chapters are all related in subject and purpose.

Some of the same illustrations are given in more than one chapter when they serve to clarify more than one point.

Lloy A. Kniss

CONTENTS

THE BIBLE SPEAKS

1. *Gen. 7:1*–And the LORD said unto Noah, Come thou and all thy house into the ark; for thee have I seen righteous before me in this generation.
2. *Gen. 18:19*–For I know him, that he will command his children and his household after him, and they shall keep the way of the LORD, to do justice and judgment; that the LORD may bring upon Abraham that which he hath spoken of him.
3. *Deut. 6:6-9*–And these words which I command thee this day, shall be in thine heart. And thou shalt teach them diligently unto thy children, and shalt talk of them when thou sittest in thine house, and when thou walkest by the way, and when thou liest down, and when thou risest up. And thou shalt bind them for a sign upon thine hand, and they shall be as frontlets between thine eyes. And thou shalt write them upon the posts of thy house, and on thy gates.
4. *Prov. 22:6*–Train up a child in the way he should go: and when he is old, he will not depart from it.
5. *Prov. 22:15*–Foolishness is bound in the heart of a child; but the rod of correction shall drive it far from him.
6. *Prov. 13:24*–He that spareth his rod hateth his son; but he that loveth him chasteneth him betimes.
7. *Prov. 23:13*–Withhold not correction from the child: for if thou beatest him with the rod, he shall not die.
8. *Prov. 23:14*–Thou shalt beat him with the rod, and shalt deliver his soul from hell.
9. *Prov. 29:15*–The rod and reproof give wisdom: but a child left to himself bringeth his mother to shame.
10. *Eph. 6:4*–And, ye fathers, provoke not your children to wrath: but bring them up in the nurture and admonition of the Lord.

As we were crossing the Indian Ocean one evening, we were being treated to a magnificent sight. The water was smooth as glass and at the surface were floating thousands of jelly fish, each one perhaps eight inches in diameter. These fish were of various colors—white, blue, green, red, pink, yellow. The sight was most gorgeous.

I had a special friend among the passengers, with whom I had become acquainted on this trip. He was a very well-read man, but he was an agnostic. This did not hinder my love for him, and we often conversed about serious matters. We stood side by side at the rail taking in the interesting sight.

As we were admiring the beauty of it all, he remarked, "Isn't this wonderful?" I replied, "Yes, and to think these things all just came about by themselves!" This angered him and he turned at once and went to his cabin. I felt badly for I had been very untactful. Nevertheless, in a few hours he returned again. I had not lost his friendship. Some time later he said to me, "I wish I could believe like you do. I know that you are happier than I am."

Let us lead our children to faith in God, then they too will be happy.

1

Faith in God

The waning of faith in God among any people and the deterioration of character run hand in hand.

One of the most natural things for a very young child is to believe in God. Such a child may not realize he believes, but he is just conscious of the fact. In fact, it is doubtful that any one, regardless of age, can honestly say he does not believe in God's existence. We want the child to have more than an intellectual belief in God. He must learn to depend on God, and he must be conscious of his relation to God. This must be taught, and is easily caught from God-fearing parents.

The child's very first god is his father. Everyone is born with the instinct to look up to one higher than himself. This helps every person to find his proper relation to others in his life. The child in a Christian home has an early advantage.

In every Christian home, family worship should be a regular practice. A child in such a home sees and hears his father and mother kneel and talk to God every day from the time he is an infant. That child will never need proof that God exists. Then as he grows older, he makes the transition from his father to God in such a natural way that he isn't conscious of the change of faith. All this combination of persons, events, physical and mental development, and God's Spirit working together to make a child God-conscious is one of the marvels of God's provision for us. If the child learns to respect his father as the authority to be obeyed, he will hold the same attitude toward God.

The responsibility and the opportunity of being a father, in this respect, is tremendous.

The Bible, which is God's Word, must be given first place in the home as far as any reading or source of information is concerned. If the parents have regarded the Bible this way, the child will likely do the same. The Bible is to be read, rather than kept in a prominent place as an ornament or a mere symbol. One family I knew had an expensive Bible with a satin ribbon tied around it with a large beautiful bow, lying nicely on top of a television set. This use of a Bible seems to be something like using the Lord's name in vain.

Children should be taught always to thank God for food and ask Him to bless it to their good. This attitude and practice of the family should be so regular and natural that children will never forget it. The importance of a child's hearing his parents pray cannot be overstressed. Of course, children should be trained early to pray audibly in the family. Memorized children's prayers may have a place for a time in a child's life, but the child should begin early to pray extemporaneously, that is, from the heart.

It has happened too often that when a child's praying sounds cute or amusing to older people, they remark about it or laugh afterward. This is always wrong. Regardless how childish a child's prayer may sound to older ones, they should never mention it or smile over it.

The question to ask when some course of action is discussed should not be, "What will people think of this?" but, "What does God think of it?" This helps children to know God is feared and honored above all else. A thing is right or wrong on the basis of God's Word, not what man thinks or says about it.

Strictly observing the first day of the week as the Lord's day also helps to stabilize a child's faith in God. Every day should be lived for God, of course, but to be very conscientious in keeping the Lord's day holy and free from unnecessary work or business says something to a growing child that will keep him conscious of God. It is obvious that increasing crime, godlessness, and desecration of the Lord's Day are closely related. One can hardly say that one of these alone is the cause of the other evil conditions, but they are certainly involved together. Don't send your child to the store or stop for ice cream on Sunday. Stop at a restaurant for a meal on Sunday only when it is really necessary. Sunday discussions of sale bargains are not only unnecessary, but detrimental, to the child's faith. One must, however, avoid fanatical extremes that create a legalistic attitude. This, however, is not very often the case. No one in the family should ever find it necessary to ask on Sunday morning, "Are we going to church today?" unless there are conditions that prohibit it. Going to church should be so regular that it is one of the good, unquestioned habits of a family.

Every parent should be concerned for the conversion of the child when he comes to the age of accountability. No evangelist or pastor can as naturally and as artfully lead a young person to yield himself to Christ as Lord and to receive the new birth experience as a wise, deeply spiritual father or mother. Evangelists are needed for children of Christian homes when parents are incapable because of lack of Bible knowledge or of spiritual depth to lead their children to conversion. The father who provided the necessities of life for the child, and the mother who nursed the child as an infant and told him Bible stories as a child, are truly the logical ones to lead a young person to Christ. When parent-child relationships are as they should be, children, youth, and even adults will naturally come to parents for counsel, especially in spiritual matters.

In the spring of 1942 our family was returning from India. At that time some of the most intense fighting on the seas in World War II was in progress. We were passengers on a large ocean liner which was used as a troop ship and had taken soldiers to Bombay. Now on its return trip to New York, it carried fifteen hundred passengers, all of whom were civilians or ex-soldiers. About four hundred of these were missionaries returning home.

No lights were allowed on the ship because of the constant danger of being found by enemy submarines. Since reading was impossible after dark, about eight hundred of the passengers gathered on deck each evening for a period of singing. One missionary led us in singing hymns and gospel songs for an hour or more each evening.

Our leader knew a great many songs by memory and we sang different songs each night except the first one, "Jesus Saviour, Pilot Me," and the last one, "Abide With Me." These two we sang each evening. We sang into the dark of the night with water all around us, starry skies over us, concern in our minds, trust in our hearts, and the Spirit of God among us. These periods were times of deep reverence and of real worship which I will never forget.

2

Reverence

Reverence results from the combination of a recognition of God's presence, a healthy fear of God, and a humility of spirit. It is respect for God, for His Word, for His creation, for His protection and care, and for His great power and knowledge.

Reverence in church can and should be taught to a child when quite young. It is natural and normal for a young infant to cry in church. A child under five or six cannot understand *why* he must be quiet in church. He won't know what reverence means. But long before he is five he can learn that in certain places he must be quiet. Some people think it wrong to try to make a little "wiggler" sit still for any length of time. This is a false notion. If you wait until your child is old enough to understand why he should sit still in church, you will have lost the best time to start him.

A very young child can learn self-discipline. Reverence in church, even for older people, requires self-discipline. We don't automatically sit still just when we find out why we should sit still. Much less a child, who understands less.

An infant crying in church is showing a sign of some need. If the crying persists too long, the mother takes him out and takes care of the need. A child of eight months or more can be trained to be quiet in church. At least, by that time such training should begin. He can know what is required of him long before he can talk in sentences. The mother who knows her child will know whether he is crying from discomfort or because he wants his way. Once when

15

our first boy was eight months old, he cried in church, obviously because he wanted to have his own way about something, and he persisted until his mother took him out. He stopped crying as soon as his mother started out with him. When she was outside, she held him tightly and did not let him wiggle. He didn't like this so he cried again, but she continued this for a time. When she relaxed her hold on him, he stopped crying. Then she talked to him to let him know she loved him. As she talked, she took him back into the church and sat down with him on her lap. After a little while he still wanted his own way and cried again so she took him out and repeated the same treatment. After she took him back in again, he still cried. Taking him out the third time, she did the same thing. When she took him in that time, he was quiet, and she had very little trouble with him in church after that. He couldn't talk, but he understood what his mother wanted. It took three treatments before he learned it was less "fun" to be taken out than to stay in. Some people would object and call this cruelty. But it was not. It was less painful for him then than it would have been later to break an established habit. Little children have a built-in capacity to take some pressures without future ill effects.

Certainly that little fellow didn't know what reverence was, but when he became old enough to know, he had little difficulty acting reverently in church. He had learned self-discipline.

Some mothers take toys or picture books to church to keep their little ones entertained. This is legitimate for young children who cannot understand. But when toys are brought to church, they must be only noiseless ones. Anything that makes noise when it drops is not appropriate. When a child is old enough to play with toy cars or trucks, he is old enough to be quiet in church without toys. Once a boy had a toy hammer in church and he played carpenter on the church bench. This type of toy has no place in a church meeting. Sometimes children as old as fifteen years read books during the service. Such things are out of place. (The fault in this case could be in the preacher, but this does not excuse the child.)

Reverence in the home is equally important and should be learned by the child at the same time he learns it in church. Reverence is reaction to God's presence, not a formality for a certain place; however, the details of reverent behavior in the home are not the same as those in church.

Remembering the earlier definition for "reverence" as a certain attitude resulting from combined fear of God, humility, and consciousness of God's presence, we should readily see the importance of training little children to be reverent in the home.

Of course a child cannot be taught reverence in the home when his parents become irritated and shout at each other or at the children, and in other ways give vent to anger. The parents themselves must be Christians and be reverent.

Each parent should help the children to respect the other parent. This is natural when the parents are well-mated and well-adjusted to each other.

However, parents are also human, and the father or mother might require something of the child that is unjust or questionable. This is not good and should be avoided. But the damage to the child even in such a case would be less than the damage caused by the other parent if he should take the child's part and let him know it, either secretly or before the other parent. Parents must come to an understanding with each other in the absence of the child. The parent who dealt unjustly with the child should be the one to do any explaining or apologizing to the child that might be needed. Let it be said that there are times when apologies must be made to children. If a young child has been made to believe that his father or his mother is perfect, he will become disillusioned when he is old enough to understand, and the shock will then cause him to lose confidence. A child who is old enough to talk and do a bit of reasoning can learn that his parents are human and yet continue to respect and reverence them. This will make the proper situation in which the child can naturally believe in and reverence God whom he cannot see or feel physically, knowing, however, God is perfect and can make no mistakes.

A motto seen in many homes is, "Christ is the head of this house." The child is told that the Bible is God's Word. When he sees parents disregarding God's Word, the motto becomes a lie. This is not reverence.

Whining, grumbling, pouting, scolding, screaming, going into temper tantrums, refusing to talk, retaliating and other like reactions are the opposite of reverence. Probably all children will react in one or more of these ways at times because they are human and have depraved natures, but the parents must do all they can to help the child overcome these things. One thing a small child sometimes does when he is displeased with what his mother requires of him is to strike her or fight back. Mostly this is the result of some failure in the past when the child was not trained in respect or reverence. This is a sign that the parent should do something about this now. It is difficult to say what a parent should do in such cases since children are different and the causes for their reactions are varied.

However, some things are pertinent. The parent must not simply become a partner in a two-way fight. Any anger that is aroused must be controlled. Love must motivate the parent's response, and firmness is indispensable. The age of the child must be considered. Probably when a very young child strikes his mother or father, the best thing for the child would be for the parent to strike him, hitting him hard enough that he will not want to strike back. If he cries, let him cry, especially if his crying is sincere. But if he

18

cries only to impress the parent, it should not be allowed to go on. This kind of treatment may not work for an older child.

When children grow up in a home where every morning, evening, and meal time the family prays to their heavenly Father, they already have a good start in reverence everywhere, whether in the home, church, school, store, the woods, or the field.

Reverence in private living is something very important that a child should learn. A certain mother was in the house with her little daughter when she saw a neighbor lady coming toward the house. She exclaimed to her daughter, "There comes that troublesome Jane again!" But when the neighbor knocked at the door, the mother said to her as she opened the door, "I'm so glad to see you, come in." This made a deep impression on her daughter. It was saying to her, in effect, you can think what you want to in private about your neighbor, or about God, or your parents, but you must always put on a good front when you meet them. This mother very effectively taught irreverence, by example, to her young daughter.

My father once told me about an experience when he was a teen-age boy. He came to his father and began telling him something unfavorable about a neighbor. As soon as his father knew he was telling something that was damaging to the neighbor, he shook his finger at the boy and he didn't need to say a word. The boy stopped in the middle of his sentence and said no more. In that kind of home the young man grew up to respect parents, neighbors, and God in his own private thinking. This was good old German discipline in a German Lutheran home, perhaps a hundred years ago. They probably never had mottoes on the wall, but they had reverence in the home, and in their private thought life.

The spirit of reverence must be instilled in the child's mind as he views God's handiwork in nature. This is probably caught more than taught as the child observes parents who reverence God in these matters. As we see works of God in nature, we are made to praise and thank Him, whether we see a beautiful flower unfolding, a giant tree weathering the storm, the responsive smile of a baby, the behavior of barnyard fowl and animals, or whether we hear a wren happily singing, or see the law of nature working when a heavy rock is moved by a long lever. There are thousands of such bits of nature that mean much to us as we observe them with reverence to their Creator. People who don't know the true God will worship the creature, not the Creator, as they see flowers, trees, rocks, animals, and natural forces and instincts. Take children on nature hikes and use the opportunity to teach them about their Creator. This will help them to harbor clean thoughts instead of the vulgar.

Reverence in social mingling with other people is a mark of geniune Christian character.

Very young children, even before they know the meaning of it all, can be trained to have proper respect for God in the presence of other people, young or old. Why is it that so many people actually feel embarrassed to talk about God or religion when present with other people? Why are many people unable to pray audibly in a public gathering? Why are people unwilling to bow their heads even in silent prayer before eating a meal in a restaurant?

Isn't it because they are brought up in homes where their parents had the same problem? Or perhaps the parents simply failed to train their children to be reverent.

There are two kinds of people who are bold in talking about God or religion when they are among other people. The one kind talks religion freely to impress others with their spirituality, or they may simply be reckless and willing to talk about any subject that comes up. The other kind will freely talk about God because they feel at home in such conversation and know God is greater than anyone else, because they have experienced Him.

Again it should be said that regular family worship in the home will foster the proper attitude in children.

A two-year-old should be ready at any time to answer the question, "Who made you?" A teen-ager should always be ready to pray in a group when he is asked to do so.

Parents should talk freely to each other and to their children about God and His goodness and what He does. God should not only be someone we talk about on Sundays or in church. His name in a Christian family should be as familiar as the name of anyone in the family. Children in the home, who are conscious of God's presence, are secure and are being prepared to face difficult things in life.

Reverence to God and respect for friends, neighbors, and strangers are not the same, but such reverence and respect are most certainly related. Young children should never be exposed to gossip about other people. They should not be allowed to indulge in unfavorable talk about playmates.

A little boy might come in and say, "Jimmy hit me." The wise mother might then say, "Well, you know God loves Jimmy and you too, so why don't you just forgive him and play again?" Or she may say "Did you do something to him that wasn't nice?" If he did, then he should go and apologize to Jimmy. The boy who complained to his mother should be kept conscious all the while that God sees everything that goes on.

Parents should guard against the feeling that their children are better than other children. If other children are not trained as well as theirs, they should remember that if they were thus trained, they would be like their own are. A sympathetic attitude is always much better than a superior attitude. One of the greatest mistakes mothers make is to feel that their children would never tell a lie, but that other children do. This attitude can make social misfits of children for their entire lives.

Reverence in school is pretty well mastered when the right attitudes are developed in the home, in church, and in society. You have all three of these relationships in school. It is well-known that a boy's conduct and demeanor in school is a reliable index of conditions in his home and his church.

Parents should not give the child the idea that school is a place to go to have a good time only. He should be aware that school requires work and is something God gives us so we can learn how to live better and more happily. The child who is conscious of God's presence at home and in church will adjust more easily in school. He will relate more properly to his teacher and to other children. Parents who pray with the child just before sending him off to school will help him immensely to that end.

Many Sunday afternoons in my boyhood days were spent at home in our living room with my mother. We lived on an isolated farm on a hill. This was quite different from living in a city where one could see other people by merely looking out the window.

My heart wells up in thankfulness as I recall how my mother would get the large family Bible with its many colored pictures related to Bible times and call us four boys to stand around her as she turned the pages of the Bible on her lap. She told us the story of each picture as she turned those large leaves. She never got through the Bible at one sitting, but she covered the Bible more than once over a long period of time.

I am sure that this is where I first began to find interest in and to have a love for the Bible. I thank my heavenly Father for Christian parents who did so much in making the Bible a real part of my life. I am sure I can say nothing better to my readers than to suggest that you do as my mother did. TEACH THE BIBLE TO YOUR LITTLE ONES.

3

Love for the Bible

In this day when more and more people are losing faith in the Bible, and many are out to destroy all the old established institutions and foundations of life, mankind is facing the possibility of total chaos. This is because the Bible—the one and only thing in this world that is basic, true, unchangeable, and ultimately reliable—is also being included in this effort to do away with these things.

We thank God for the Bible. It is one thing He gave us that has weathered every storm, is still the basic source of all right teaching, and is life-giving and life-sustaining. Our fear is not that God's Word will be destroyed, but that men will destroy themselves by forsaking or denying God's Word. One of the first essentials in child training is to instill in the child a love for God's Word.

Effective training in respecting and loving God's Word begins in infancy. If the mother does not possess love for the Bible, then she cannot instill love for it in her child. If you object to the word *infancy* in the former statement, you do not understand how early a child is affected by the mother's attitudes.

One summer morning a salesman came to the open door of a home to present his product. The young mother of the home was sitting on a rocker inside the open door nursing her baby and reading aloud from the Bible. "Oh!" said the salesman, "Reading the Bible to your baby?" He meant this for a joke. She replied, "Yes, sir, that is just what I am doing." The salesman lost in his first effort to try to win her confidence. She was so wise that he must have felt foolish.

This young mother was right. While the infant was receiving bodily nourishment from his mother, he also heard the voice of his mother reading the Bible. As this was repeated daily, he associated the pleasant experience of receiving nourishment with the sound of his mother's voice. This created love for and confidence in his mother's voice. When the child grew to be able to understand, his mother told him stories and read from the Bible to him. This naturally sounded so right to him that he accepted and loved it. You can't begin too early in your infant's life to develop in him love for the Bible. The mother is the most logical and the most effective teacher for the young child, if she is a true Christian.

Telling Bible stories to children is important. My wife made much use of "Egermeier's Bible Stories" in reading stories to our children. The stories are written in simple language and are true to the Biblical text. They never grew old to the children, and I believe helped to develop a love for the Bible in their hearts.

In many things it is true that "familiarity breeds contempt," but in the case of God's Word the very opposite is true. With the Bible, familiarity increases love. Sometimes people speak of being "Gospel-hardened." No child will become "Gospel-hardened" from hearing it often. When they seem hardened to it, the fault isn't in being familiar with it, but perhaps in listening to its being presented in an uninteresting way or in unpleasant circumstances. The following two points will support this thought.

The Bible must never be used as a means only to entertain the child. Reading will certainly entertain, but to use the Bible for the sole purpose of entertainment cheapens it. This would also destroy the opportunity to develop a reverent attitude toward the Bible. We should use it in the way the Bible itself says it should be used. The Scripture is "profitable for doctrine, for reproof, for correction, for instruction." With every Bible story the

26

mother should interpret the moral or the teaching of the story. The young child's mind will readily respond to this kind of treatment of the stories. When older children or teen-agers begin to complain, "You are always preaching to me," it is not because of telling the morals of the stories, but because of having lost communication from some other cause.

Every child is instinctively religious from brith. This should be cultivated to develop a special love for the Bible. So very much depends on the attitude of the parents as to whether the child or the teen-ager will be "soured" on being taught spiritual truths, or whether he will accept and cherish them. The parent's part in this matter is extremely important.

Love for the Bible cannot be taught by a parent who does not love it. This also is caught rather than taught.

Never use the Bible to threaten children when they misbehave. When a mother tells her boy who lied, "The Bible says that liars go to hell"; or says to a child who won't tell, "Be sure your sin will find you out"; or to a teen-age boy who got into trouble with the law, "Whatsoever a man soweth, that shall he also reap"; or to a young child who slaps another, "Now Jesus won't love you" (which isn't true); she is making wrong use of the Bible, and her children will not learn to love God's Word. Such Scriptural quotations are true, but when they are used in wrong situations or in wrong ways, then harm is done, rather than good.

One should never make a child read a chapter from the Bible or memorize a verse from the Bible for punishment. This is sometimes done by well-meaning parents, but it can turn a child against the Bible. It should be obvious that this is not proper punishment for a child. To punish a child with something he likes to do isn't punishment. It is punishment only when a child must do something he doesn't like to do. To make a child read a chapter or memorize a verse for punishment would be assuming that the child hates to do this, and in this way the child would be led to hate the Bible rather than to love it.

Don't change or skip parts of the Bible when teaching children just because they can't understand it. Don't omit reading even any single passage which seems to border on obscenity by our standards. There are no obscene passages in the Bible, but our present society has created some artificial standards and ideas of morality which make some passages seem too candid. All passages should be read as one comes to them and then explained. In some such passages, the opportunity to give some honest and pure sex information to children presents itself in most natural settings.

The omitting of some passages in order to evade an explanation or to avoid a seemingly undesirable thought or expression will undermine the child's faith in the Bible. It also will arouse the curiosity of the child when he knows something was skipped. He will later read it for himself, but likely in the wrong frame of mind.

The Bible must never be used by the child as a toy. There is nothing sacred about the paper and ink that compose the book, but the Word of God is sacred. To use a Bible as a toy would seem to belittle the Word of God and make it less respected by the child as he grows. It is a good practice to let the young child carry a New Testament along to church, even before he is able to read it. If the superintendent is alert, he will see that the children get to use the Testaments in some way while in Sunday school. It may be singing the song that ends by holding up the Bible and singing "My Bible and I." The Bible is not a toy which can be lightly handled in play, neither is it a fetish or charm that is too sacred to be touched by children's hands.

As soon as a child can read, he should be given his own Bible. The child should be encouraged to read from the Bible regularly, and know that one doesn't have a Bible as an ornament or a symbol. If the parents read regularly, enjoy it, and talk to each other about what they have read, the children will learn naturally to want to read it.

With small children, rewards can be useful in motivating them to memorize verses or chapters.

Children should be encouraged to take their Bibles along to church and Sunday school and follow the teaching they hear there. Services would have no meaning if it were not for the Bible, so what is unusual about carrying a Bible to church? It is rather unusual not to carry it.

I knew a Christian in India who was highly esteemed in the church. But he didn't prove to be what he should have been in some respects. He would go to the market place to purchase supplies for his family and sometimes would take his aged mother with him. On one such occasion, he met a man who was a casual acquaintance. The friend asked him who the old woman was. He replied that she was his servant. He was so ashamed of his mother that he dishonored her. And then he made her carry his purchases while he walked home empty-handed.

Let us pray God to keep us from being ashamed of our parents. Even though some parents may not be the best parents, they should nevertheless be respected.

4

Respect for Parents

True respect for parents is better commanded by their character than demanded by them. Each parent must possess a measure of self-respect, and the parents must have real respect for each other.

Parents must possess real respect for their children also. A child is not a mere vassal or bond-servant belonging to the parent. He is also a person. He is an entity with his own rights. A wise parent who recognizes this will receive respect from the child also.

A beggar came to our home in India leading a monkey on a chain. The monkey performed for its master just as it had been trained. All of its performances were for the master's benefit. The monkey had no ambitions of its own, and the two got along well because the man was the master and the monkey was a monkey.

A certain mother always had her little girl sing for her company. Every time a neighbor or friend came to visit the mother, the daughter could expect to be called upon to show off. One day the mother arranged a tea-party for her daughter by having some other little girls come to play. The girls had their party in a room by themselves while the mother was working in the kitchen. One time during the party, the little girl came to the kitchen to call her mother to sing for her girl friends. It was then that the mother realized she did wrong in asking her daughter to sing every time she had callers.

Parents who would train their children to respect them should observe the following principles.

Parents must be firm, but not mere dictators. The line between the two is thin, but important. The dictator works from the basis of his own ego; the firm parent insists on compliance for the good of his child.

It doesn't take a child long to sense when a parent doesn't mean what he says. It is better not to forbid a child to leave the yard, than to forbid him and then ignore it if he disobeys. It is, of course, necessary to forbid when there is danger, but then it must be enforced.

It is good when the child knows his parent's wishes about a matter without being told every time. But when the parent says what he wants and the child gets the impression the parent doesn't care whether or not he obeys, then the way is being paved for a criminal career.

Strictness fosters respect. Have you ever heard someone say that a person was too strict with his children? That is not true judgment. Parents don't lose the respect of their children by being strict. However, strictness without love is very damaging. If the parent doesn't enforce his commands, he need not hope for respect from his child. Dictators get obedience, but not real respect.

I have often heard persons express high regard and respect for their parents who were very strict with them as children. One reason for so much insecurity among teen-agers today is that their parents are not strict enough.

Genuine love for the child is essential if the child is to respect his father and mother. The baby must be cuddled by the parents if he is to grow up to respect them. For small children, physical expressions of affection are quickly understood. "Coddling" sounds almost like "cuddling," but it is really making babies out of children by over-indulgence and pampering. This is destructive in character. It is not only *small* children who need much love. Love is always a requisite, regardless of age, but it needs to be expressed in ways suitable to the ages. Parents must work and play in games with growing children.

Genuine love is characterized by the constant desire to give one's self to another without the thought of receiving in return. When one's love depends on the other's love for him, then it has lost its genuineness. God so loved the world (which did not love Him), that He gave. . . .

Agreement between parents is also essential in gaining respect from the children. From this angle, the training of children begins with the courtship days of their parents. The young man and woman who contemplate marriage need to consider any basic differences in their ideals and purposes in life.

Such differences should by all means influence their decision whether to marry or not. When important differences persist through married life, then it is practically impossible to rear children who respect the parents and feel secure.

I personally know a family in which the girls wanted something the father did not want them to have. The mother was in agreement with the girls and helped them get it. One day the girls were working with the forbidden thing, when Mother spied Father coming toward the house. Quickly she said, "Girls put that away, Daddy's coming." The girls quickly tucked things away and tried to appear innocent when Daddy came in. These attitudes were kept up, and when the girls were grown, they had very little respect for either one of the parents, especially the mother.

Some differences in opinions and standards can be expected in any married couple. Major and basic differences should be avoided or resolved. Minor ones can be taken care of by either parent conceding to the other. Usually the mother should submit to the father. Then the adverse influence on the children can be minimized.

Such differences as religious faith, philosophy of life, or great differences in background should not be found in married couples.

Parents must level with the child. There needs to be

fairness and justice in every dealing with the child. I knew a father who promised his son fifty cents if he would take a dose of castor oil before going to bed. The boy agreed and took the oil. The father laid the half dollar on the boy's dresser, telling him that in the morning he could get it. The next morning when the boy got out of bed, the half dollar was gone. The father had taken it. When the boy told me the story he was grown up and laughed it off, but I know there wasn't much love evident in their father-and-son relationship.

A grown young man was in trouble with the law because he committed robbery. The father was deeply troubled about this and said to the boy, "Didn't I always teach you to do better?" The boy replied, "I remember a time or two when you got too much change from a store clerk and you kept it, so you are not much better, are you?"

Some people think a father weakens his influence when he apologizes to his child for a mistake. This is not true. When a father owes an apology to his child, he must by all means make it. It will make up for the bad influence from his mistake.

When parents knowingly violate the rules of their church, they are effectively undermining any respect the child has for them. It should be repeated that true respect for parents is commanded, not demanded.

Never use the family's reputation as a lever to bring your child into line. Children should never be corrected by telling them they are bringing a bad name on the family. Many times ministers' children were discouraged because their father, though meaning well, told them that people were watching them.

Expect your children to be true to your standards, but don't express surprise when they do something wrong. Just remember you were a child too. When a father is surprised about a child's misconduct, he reveals his failure to understand the child. This is not saying, however, that the child's behavior should be overlooked or excused. It seems almost a paradox, but the child will be disappointed if you are surprised at his misconduct or if you ignore it and fail to correct him.

A child feels secure when he has parents who understand why he misbehaved, who know what is right, and require obedience to the right. Any child who has the privilege of growing up under such parents is the possessor of a heritage of great value that can't be estimated.

Some parents claim their children would never tell a lie. When stories of trouble from their children and from the neighbor's children conflict, it is always (in their mind) the neighbor's children who lie. The child growing up under such "protective" parents will be seriously maladjusted for life.

Let us as elders remember how secure we feel under a God who knows our weaknesses, who reminds us when we go wrong, and who gives us grace to repent and do right instead of wrong.

A middle-aged neighbor once came to me complaining that he asked my three-year-old boy to do something and he refused to obey. I made apology to my neighbor, but never said one word about it to my boy, who was not present when the neighbor complained. I knew he would have obeyed me if I had asked him to do that same thing. The boy was on the right track for his age; I didn't want him to obey just anyone who might ask something of him. I have no criticism for a child of two or three who shakes his head negatively when I ask him to come to me. This is natural and even good. If he would do it to his father, however, I would have different thoughts. Didn't Jesus say about his sheep, "A stranger will they not follow, . . . for they know not the voice of strangers"? This is reasonable, right, and safe. However, real respect for others must be instilled in the child's mind. "Respect for" and "obedience to" are not always synonymous.

5

Respect for Others

This is not to be repetitious of the preceding chapter, because respect for parents is different from respect for others in general.

Let your very young child mingle and play with others of the same age. I have often seen that children in comparatively large families in which brothers and sisters were born close together are the best adjusted in society when they grow up. The social instinct is one of the first to show up in a very young child. You have no doubt noticed how easily a baby will smile at another baby that is held close to him. That ready response to another of the same age is a sign of health and normalcy. Care must be exercised when young children play together lest they injure each other by scratching with their nails, or poking fingers into each other's eyes. They do such things before they are old enough to realize the consequences. Along with the good instincts of sociability and curiosity, come other instincts such as revenge or self-preservation which will hurt and mark the victims. Here some parents think they should not interfere, but let children fight it out or learn by experience. This is not correct, regardless of what some psychologists say. Children are human, not animals. They are plagued with depravity of human nature and act like animals when left to themselves. To thus leave them to themselves would train them to be hard neighbors. Young children must be restrained by those who are much older and stronger. This way they learn what is right and what is wrong for them. Some children grow up feeling it is wrong to take meanness from others without fighting back.

Train children to share toys and "goodies" with others. The beginning of such training will be between the mother and the child. Little ones can understand when parents talk to them, long before they themselves can talk. Suppose a little one is given a toy which he likes. The wise mother will stay by the child for a while and show him that she is glad he has such a nice toy. Soon she will hold out her hand and ask him to give her the toy. If the child gives her the toy, she should play with it. If it is a rattle, she should shake it and show her enjoyment over it, getting the child to enjoy it with her. After a little while, she should give it back and enjoy watching the child play with it. This kind of exchange should be frequent.

If the child refuses to give the toy to his mother, she should not take it by force. By some ingenuity of her own, she should persuade the child to give it up until he has done it often enough that he sees the benefit in it. Then he will do it gladly.

A well-adjusted adult will use all legitimate ways of securing what he wants or needs without demanding, or fighting for it. Demanding things for one's self is very juvenile. When one gets anything he needs by legitimate means, he will thoroughly enjoy it. If he doesn't receive what he wants, he will not be upset. When he sees another person getting things, he will rejoice with the other person even though he didn't get what he wanted.

Our aim with young children is always to lead them to maturity, and to help them form habits that identify mature persons. Some people say you can't put old heads on young shoulders. That is very true in many ways, but you also cannot expect young heads to grow to maturity while they are pampered either on young or old shoulders. This is the principal reason so many grown people act like spoiled children.

I am sure your child can learn to be happy when someone else receives something.

Help growing children to see good in others. This can be done best when children are two years old or more. The best way to start children in this matter is for parents to be careful in their own attitude toward other people. It is never good to talk unfavorably about people that are known by the family. Criticism or accusing talk about teachers, church leaders, playmates, officials, and others should never be engaged in by parents in the presence of children. The only exception to this rule would be where children are old enough to understand and need to be warned against strangers who might try to get them into their cars or befriend them for evil purposes. The reason for all this is to develop in the child the attitude of seeing good in others rather than being critical or fearful of them.

The sense of obligation or indebtedness to other people must be developed in a child if he is to be well adjusted. Some children are pampered, and everything they want is given to them or done for them by their parents. Such children feel the world owes them a living. Everyone with whom they deal is indebted to them as they see it.

Some parents live only for their children and themselves. This results in what was just described. However, the parents who live first for God and then for other people who are in need and who take their children with them on this inspiring and enjoyable course of life do a far greater service for their children than those who live solely for their children. Such children grow up with the sense of call to give themselves to others for the glory of God. They will not be without purpose in life and will become an asset to any society. They will do more for their country than those who enter politics, join the army, or become rulers and governors. The highest aim in life is to love God with the whole heart, soul, strength, and mind, and our neighbors as ourselves. To train up a child to have this high purpose for life is the good parent's task.

The sense of property must be learned by the child who

is to be a good member of any society. At first, a child is not able to ask, "Is this mine or yours?" When you hold him, he will not hesitate to grab your glasses, grasp your nose or your ear. When he is old enough to play with toys, he will hold to what appeals to him, whether it belongs to him or someone else. He gives no thought as to whose it is. He just likes it and wants it.

For young children this is normal and no one takes exception to it. However, if this attitude persists after he is three, there is cause for alarm. Somewhere a mistake was made. Children can learn that some things are theirs and some are not. Some learn only because of the reaction by those whose property was taken. They learn not to take another's toy because they don't want to get hit. This is accommodation, not training; it will only hold as long as the owner has the power to keep things from him. Some people grow to physical maturity and still lack the sense of property. I know a man who was buying a house and lot. He still owed five hundred dollars, but was allowed to move into the house before paying it. The creditor came to him and asked for the five hundred dollars. The debtor replied saying, "Yes, I owe it to you, but make me pay it. If you go to court, then I'll pay." This debtor lacked a proper sense of property. He was a deliberate thief. It is important that children are trained to respect other people's property.

Then, there are people who wouldn't cheat a neighbor out of a dime, but wouldn't hesitate to defraud the government out of a hundred or a thousand dollars. This shows a very distorted sense of property.

If a very young child insists on keeping someone else's toy, and fights or cries for it, the parent must exercise his role as an older, stronger person. If necessary, he must take the toy from the child's hand by force. He must do it kindly and gently, and not mind the child's crying. This must be done consistently, not just at times. Being forced to do this while he is too young to understand, will train

40

the child to do right. This is the proper way to train the young child.

As the child grows in age, stature, and mind, the parent must strive to develop the child's conscience so that when he violates someone else's property rights, he will feel condemned. The basic principle here is love and respect for others. When a child has this love for others, he will not violate their property rights very easily, nor fight for rights to his own property. This is not making a child "wishy-washy" or "easy-going." In reality, it takes a character that is extra strong to cheerfully take the spoiling of one's goods. It takes a person who has greater values in reserve to not feel threatened when his material possessions are in danger.

When a young child is taught the sense of property in the right way, he will not commit arson later, go around breaking windows, or steal. And he will never rest after having taken too much change.

Respect for age is a positive quality in a properly trained child. In America we are guilty in this matter. Old people are despised and their counsel is often not regarded. There are times when aged people's counsel is not good because they have become senile or have lost some reasoning powers; but even while declining their counsel, young people should always hold them in respect.

Little children want to become older. They can't wait until they are sixteen or twenty-one. Then, as soon as they are forty, they would be glad to be able to turn the clock back. When they become fifty or sixty and someone asks their age, they say ''guess.'' They hope they don't look too old, and will be guessed to be much younger.

It is certainly not being honest to wish to be considered older or younger than you really are. "Vanity and artificiality make common buddies."

A child should be taught to respect age. This attitude can also be "caught" by the child when the parent's

41

attitude toward seniors is what it should be. The child will imbibe the parents' spirit more quickly than accept their verbal teachings.

God has planned no man's life to go through good stages, then into worse stages, and again into more desirable stages. It is God's plan for every child to move out of the childhood stage into a better one, then into a still better one, and so on to the end of life. If normally lived, each age should be better than the one before, and finally; old age, if Christian, will go into a better state—with God in heaven. If children can be given this vision of advancing age, then they will respect old age even more. Their view of life will be more normal, more inspiring, and they will be more mature and useful at every age.

Never allow children to refer to their father as the "old man," or their mother as the "old woman." When a teen-ager describes his father as "old fogey," then something has slipped. Never allow children to mock or make fun of older people.

Respect for church leaders and civil officers is a must if a child is to be well-adjusted and feel secure. This was alluded to in a former section, but it deserves a fuller treatment.

When I see a police officer on the street stopping to befriend a little boy or girl, I get inspired. When I see a church leader noticing the young boys and girls in the church or holding smaller children in his arms, I know there are children and young people in that church who will respect their leaders. There are many things a leader can do which will command respect from the young rather than cause resentment toward him.

However, it is true that the key persons in bringing up a child to respect leaders are the parents of the child.

Parents must never coerce the child into obedience by scaring him with the police. Instead, they should tell their child all the good they can think of about a policeman. Then if ever a policeman has to talk to the child after he is partly grown, he will be respectful toward the policeman and will want to obey. If this is not the case, the teen-ager will be resentful or antagonistic toward the policeman.

The parent's attitude toward church leaders will do more to train the child than what the parent says in words. Many people have roast beef, pork, or chicken for Sunday dinner. But, alas! many children in this world are fed "roast preacher" after they leave church! I could name a number of families who were fed on this diet, and the children went elsewhere for security rather than to that church.

Often, when a father or mother is critical of the church leader, the underlying cause is in the parent. He may be guilty of some inconsistency himself. Then the deadly combination of the example of an inconsistent parent and a preacher in whom he has no confidence almost certainly wrecks the child's life.

Where is the energetic, optimistic and clear-thinking young person who would risk his life to a church which he heard being constantly criticized by his parents? Dear young parents, the precious young jewel God gave you to take care of and train is a great responsibility. Be careful of your attitude toward your church.

I was once in a community for a series of meetings and was invited to supper by one of the lay members of the church. This man was a farmer with eight or nine boys, ranging in age from eleven down. When all arrived in the home, the father pulled a chair over beside the sheet-iron, wood-burning stove and invited me to be seated. He then turned to the boys and said, "I'll do the chores this evening myself. You boys stay here with Brother Kniss." Then the father said to me, "Whenever a minister comes to our home, I always tell the boys to stay with him, and I do the work." The evening went by without any outstanding event, but now, thirty-five years later, all those boys are working in the church somewhere. A number of them are ordained ministers or deacons. The father of this family deserves consideration as a model father. He was consistent in teaching his family other things besides teaching them to respect ministers.

Young children should be taken to church regularly. They do not understand what is spoken, but they become accustomed to the sounds and sights, and they meet people, so that going to church seems the right thing to do. They get into the habit of going to church, and this is good. Much of the complaining by some young folks about being forced to go to church when they did not want to go is misplaced criticism. However, there are instances where church services are not very attractive for children. When children claim they are forced to go to church, something other than force is involved. In homes that are what they ought to be, children will want to go to church.

Charles, one of my friends in my youth, was of such personality and character that I still hold him in high esteem. What made him so admirable?

Charles gave evidence of several marks of self-respect. He never used improper or profane language. He never relished off-color jokes. He never spoke vulgarly about sex. He was never snobbish, but was always considerate of other people's feelings. He never gave evidence of low-type thinking, and he always encouraged the right. He said one time, "When I am with a girl on a date, I never do anything in the dark I wouldn't do in daylight." He was always happy and ready to help in time of need.

All these traits are marks of self-respect, for how we respect others reveals how we respect ourselves. High standards such as these may not be popular with the common run of society, but they are marks of true Christian character and are to be cultivated.

6

Self-Respect

Self-respect is not synonymous with self-esteem or selfishness. Nor are selfish pride, defensiveness and self-assertiveness compatible with self-respect. Self-confidence and a sense of security are basic in self-respect. Self-respect and the proper kind of self-love are almost the same.

The beginnings of self-respect in an adult are usually cultivated in his childhood. Real self-respect is hard to attain in later life, especially if the child's experiences were not normal. Of course, a true Christian experience in adults has remade many lives and self-respect has been achieved. But when a child is properly brought up to respect himself, he is more likely to yield himself to Christ when he reaches the age of accountability.

Self-respect in children is usually a result of the influence of self-respecting parents. Such parents have the concern for their children which is needed to instill respect in them. This is one thing that is caught as much as taught.

It is to be understood that we are not speaking about the kind of self-respect that a certain boy showed one time in Bible school when I was the superintendent. The boy needed correction, so I led him to a certain seat. The boy became angry and shouted, "Get your hands off me." Then he threatened to send his father to straighten me out. This boy thought himself to be someone, but true self-respect was badly lacking. This attitude is one of the modern day perversions in child behavior.

Children who are criticized too much will hardly develop self-respect. Too much criticism by parents or teachers will have one of two effects on children. It either undermines

47

self-confidence or causes bitterness or resentment. It will in either case cause a gap between parent and child. This critical spirit was evident in the mother who said to her daughter, "Mary, go out to the back yard and see what Johnny is doing and tell him to quit." Sometimes nervous mothers are sure that whatever the children are doing is wrong. This makes it difficult for the children to be persons. Children have been known to cry in self-pity, "Everything I do is wrong." Self-pity is not a part of self-respect.

For many young children the first words they learn to say are "no, no." They hear their mothers say this often. This can't be helped since aggressive little tots get into many forbidden things. The important thing is to know where to draw the line between necessary restraint and too much criticism. When the child hears no criticism or is never checked, he is not being treated fairly either. Here again we must avoid the extremes of being too negative or never using negatives. Wise parents will use both negatives and positives.

Continual nagging by parents or teachers breaks down self-respect. It will break down self-respect even in an adult who understands what is going on. But in a child, personality is changed without his being aware of the cause. This is even more tragic.

Proverbs 19:13 says that the contentions of a wife are as a continual dropping. This means that the nagging of a wife is like water dropping continuously. It is said that if a person would be tied in a place where water continued to drop on the same spot for a long time, the drops would finally feel like great weights. In ancient times this was used as a method of torture.

Nagging is something that older children are sometimes subject to after they are old enough to do some reasoning. When a child of this age is reluctant to obey, the parent should not keep nagging, but take time out to talk with him. If he still does not obey, then discipline of some sort should be used. Discipline is helpful, but nagging is harmful.

Children who are really loved by parents who have proper self-love, will likely develop self-respect. My wife and I were at one time responsible for a twenty-year-old girl who loved to be treated like a six-year-old in some things. She often cried because she thought we forgot to treat her like a little girl. This girl pitied herself. She was in her parents' home until she was sixteen, and had been told by her mother when she was quite young that she was an "accident" and not wanted. Her parents never really loved her as a young child, and she could not know the meaning of self-respect. She preferred us to her own father and mother. There are so many areas of life in which people suffer because they did not get the proper love and affection when they were young, or even later.

Proper or average standards of living in the home of the young child have much to do with attaining self-respect. When the child's parents are so poor that the standard of living in their home is much below the general standard of the community, the child suffers. If the standard of living in a wealthy home is much above the general community standards, the child will have a tendency to develop a spirit of pride or haughtiness. One teen-age girl from such a home said to her schoolmates, "My daddy's a big shot." She thought the police would not dare to say anything to her daddy when there was danger that they would clamp down on a certain violation in the community. This was hardly innocent self-respect.

There are other factors in a child's life, of course, which can alter the effect of living in a home of lower standards. There have been many self-respecting persons who have come from very poor homes. However, children from a poor home among others of higher living standards have one count against them, for they naturally compare themselves with others.

49

To digress a bit from our subject—some parents of young or growing children are blessed with more money than others. Very good and profitable use can be made of the extra money. They could live by standards not above their neighbors and give more to charity and missions. The children would profit in two ways. They would learn to be humble while developing self-respect, and they would learn by the parents' example to give to others in need.

Children must learn to work if our churches are to be supplied with leadership and if our country is to survive present upheavals. The need for self-respecting, hard workers who are unselfish is constantly growing.

A teen-age daughter was home for three months' vacation from school. I asked her mother why she did the cooking, dishwashing and cleaning herself while her daughter sat idly by. She said, "When my daughter comes home for only a little while, I don't think I ought to make her work." This was clearly the mother's mistake. (More will be said in another chapter about children working.) There are really very few things which will build self-respect as well as when the child knows he has not been idle while others worked.

Whether your young daughter will someday be a nurse, a secretary, or a teacher, her self-respect will be enhanced because she did her share in scrubbing floors when she was a young girl at home. Your young son may grow up to be a specialist, a technician or scientist, but he will be more dependable if he has some regular chores to perform when he is a boy in his father's home.

Children in the home should have certain privileges and opportunities similar to their peers, when these peers are also from Christian homes where beliefs and practices are in harmony with your own. Generally, if others have the privilege to attend certain social functions which are consistent with high standards of Christian conduct, then yours should have this privilege also. But if any of the privileges are not compatible with Christian standards, then the reason for not permitting your children to have them should be explained to them. They should not be allowed to attend movies, the dance hall, or other objectionable gatherings even though all their peers do. Your children should realize that they are also responsible to give a Christian witness by their participation or non-participation in community activities.

Parents will want to avoid making their children "misfits" unnecessarily. Perhaps your children's clothes will be similar to those of other children, insofar as those clothes are consistent with Christian standards of simplicity and modesty. There is no good reason to let children wear jewelry, mini-skirts, or unchristian hairdos and the like just because others do. If your children appear differently or engage in different social activities because of principle, they may help to set the standards for their peer group to follow. Your children are someone else's peers, and their influence may go much farther than they think possible. Again, there is definite value in children learning as they grow up that we are responsible to give a Christian witness in everything we do.

If other children in the community are given a regular allowance, you may want to consider giving your children one, too. When most of the other children have bicycles, then yours also might be allowed to have them. If you cannot afford this, the opportunity should be used to teach your children the dignity of living within one's means, and also that there is a difference between real necessities of life and the extras that we sometimes can use legitimately. In some settings it would be most ideal for parents of the peer group to work together in setting the standards for their children to follow.

It is good for children to have pets. There are various types of pets, some of which are dangerous and with these children need more help and supervision from their parents.

Some pets can be kept in pairs and children can raise their young and sell them. Other pets are not practical for such purposes, but in all of these children can learn lessons from nature—give and take, kindness to dumb creatures, dangers, lessons in sex, and faithful daily care and feeding. And, with all these, they can learn personal dignity and self-respect. An official who did some research among prisoners found that not one had a pet dog when he was a boy. Of course it is not good to generalize upon this, but it may be really significant.

Provisions in the home for proper privacy for the children should be made after children reach a certain age. This need shows up sometimes when children are at play. Children often do a great deal of imagining. When parents are in the room with the child as he plays, the wise parent will not let him know that he notices every detail of his play. We have all seen children glance up at their parents while they were playing, and when they saw they were being watched, they felt embarrassed. Parents should not be conspicuously watching everything a child does. There is need for a certain amount of privacy in a child's life.

A six-year-old boy in the school where I was teaching was playing by himself one day back of his parents' house in a patch of high weeds. The boy had a stick for a gun and was hunting rabbits. He cocked his gun and, holding it ready to shoot in this make-believe woods of high weeds, he quietly and carefully sneaked around some weeds looking intently at his rabbit. He was just about ready to shoot when he spied his father standing not very far away, watching him. The poor boy dropped his gun to his side and began to cry pitifully.

Can't you recall your own childhood and imagine just how the boy felt at that moment? If only the father had thought in time and quietly stepped out of the boy's sight or just looked in another direction so that the boy would not have seen him watching! That would have saved the boy a lot of pain. Not every child would cry in such a situation, but many children would have reacted similarly.

A young child is not embarrassed when his mother goes with him to the toilet. In fact at first he needs her help. But later, as he becomes able to help himself, he will gradually prefer not to have his mother with him, and she should respect this. It is also true that some of this embarrassment comes from the artificial modesty created by older people's attitudes toward the things we call private. Still, it is also natural for human beings to desire privacy. Remember, Adam and Eve hid themselves from God. We are even told that in heaven we will be clothed, so the desire for covering is not all evil.

When our children reach twelve or the teens, it is best for each one to have his own bedroom, when it is possible. There are several other good reasons for this, but privacy is sufficient reason. Even the parents should never burst into a teen-ager's bedroom without knocking and getting permission from him. Of course, if he does not give permission to enter after reasonable waiting, then there should be serious investigation. Each girl, if more than one live in the same room, should have her own dresser or drawer, with the understanding that it is private—it is hers. The same thing goes for boys.

Privacy should be provided for children, but that does not mean that parents need not know what goes on behind the children's doors. However, they should not force a door to find out. They must never peep, of course. The relationship between parents and children should be so free as to enable the parents to find out what is going on in the rooms when there is any reason for suspecting. The mutual confidence between mother and daughter should be so established that the mother knows when things are right or not in a child's behavior. Between father and son there should be no reasons to fear each other in such matters. Sometimes teen-agers are tempted to do things secretly that are wrong or improper. The parents must be very judicious in finding out. A good parent is not a secret spy nor a police to open doors. The father and mother should be priest and deaconess before whom children can be free to reveal the deepest secrets in proper ways, when such secrets need to be revealed. Parents should not demand to know every secret of a growing son or daughter.

Doing business and handling money can be profitable for children as soon as they are old enough. I wasn't yet a teen-ager when my parents allowed me to answer an ad in a magazine and order some Cloverine salve to sell. I remember how many inches "taller" I felt when I received the package containing a dozen pretty, round tins of salve that were not mine but were entrusted to me to sell for someone else. This event was really a milepost in my life.

It is very good for children to learn by experience that living is made of appointments and disappointments.

I was only ten when I was allowed to have a pair of rabbits. Father helped me cut some saplings in our woods to make a pen for them with wire netting he had bought. I raised a lot of rabbits, starting with that one pair. Some of the rabbits died. One of the does never produced young. Sometimes the rabbits dug out of the pens. I also sold some rabbits for real money! Since we lived on a farm, I had to help with the farm work and took care of my rabbits between times of working in the fields.

Last summer our two grandsons, seventeen and eighteen, built a duplex dwelling. A builder and their father helped by supervising and instructing, but they did all the work except excavating and block laying. They did the building, finishing, wiring, painting and financial record keeping, and were very enthusiastic about the project. Other boys their age ran around at night, but these boys were too tired for such activities. The building was almost completed when school started again. Children and teen-agers in the home of their parents should have the advantage of help and supervision from parents, and should learn many valuable things in such projects.

Being trusted by older people, carrying responsibilities, tasting everyday life, hard work, problems, and, of course, rewards that follow, are all worth infinitely more to growing teen-agers than running around spending money someone else has earned and having a good time. It is obvious which of the two courses will promote dignity and self-respect.

Regular attendance at Sunday school and church is a must for children who are to grow up with self-respect. The principal ingredient in building a useful life is spiritual nurture. If a person is not spiritually fitted to face life, all the secular education, moral training, learning of skills and social relations are not adequate in building a rounded-out life.

You, as parents, must take your infants to church and continue to take them as long as they are under your care and supervision.

Genuine self-respect involves human attainments, security, successful endeavor, confidence, humility, the eternal view, and other spiritual verities that come as a result of participation in Sunday school and church.

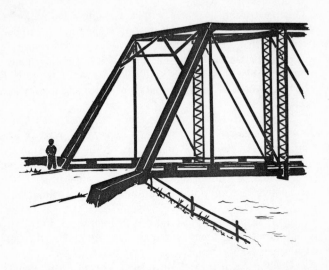

I once read an account of a father in London who took his young son along to town when he went on some business. On the way home they came to a bridge and the father recalled some business he had forgotten.

He told the boy to stand at the bridge until he returned. The father must have gone home by some other route and had completely forgotten about his son. When he arrived home at dusk, the mother asked about the boy. "Oh," said the father, "I forgot him. I must go back to the bridge to get him." Someone said, "He won't be there after all this time." "Yes he will," said the father. "I told him to stay there." When the father arrived at the bridge, he found the boy just as he had expected.

This boy had learned obedience. And the father trusted him. This was a happy situation in the end because sometime earlier the father had taught the son to obey.

7

Obedience

Obedience is at the heart of all the factors in a child's training. There is not one among God's creation who does not need to obey. The earth, stars, and all the heavenly bodies obey the Creator. Rains, seasons, rivers, winds, waves and all other inanimate creations on earth are intended to fulfill the Maker's purposes, as well as animals, birds, and other earthly creatures.

Man was created with a free will. He is the one earthly creature who can choose to obey or disobey God. If he obeys, he honors God to whom he is responsible. Only one Being, God Himself, is not subject to another.

Disobedience brings disorder and tragedy. Angels were created to serve God. Satan, because of pride, thought to exalt himself above the stars of God and to be like God. As a result, he fell and all his hosts with him. If the sun, the earth, or even the atoms of matter would fail in their orderly courses, the result would be the destruction of the universe.

When God created man, He created His most potentially dangerous earthly creature. He could decide to obey or not to obey. Adam and Eve chose to disobey, and the resulting chaos has been so great that God sent His Son to make a way for man to return to God. Those who repent and choose to live for God find order restored to their lives. All who disobey and do not repent will find their place in the lake of fire, but God's reborn children will be with Him eternally.

Obedience to God brings life; disobedience brings death.

Obedience is creative; disobedience is destructive. Obedience is godly; disobedience is satanic. Obedience brings order; disobedience brings disorder. Obedience results in blessings; disobedience brings a curse.

One of the things a child must learn is obedience. Most everyone would agree on that. The disagreement comes in the way obedience is to be taught. The weakness of many parents is that they neither teach it nor insist on it. Some simple suggestions might help in these matters.

Love is the essential ingredient in teaching obedience. Love makes the difference between a faithful and effective parent and a tyrant or a derelict. It will make the difference between willing response and forced submission. The kind of love referred to here is not the weak, sentimental so-called love that "loves" a child so much it can't punish or force him against his will. That is not love at all. The Bible tells us that the man who spares the rod hates his son. If you love your son you will use whatever means necessary to save him from future loss and tragedy. For the moment, chastening seems grievous, but afterward it brings pleasant results (Heb. 12:11).

The child will quickly sense whether obedience is required out of love for him or for some selfish motive. One father disciplined himself before correcting his son, by waiting until he was sure there was no anger present within himself. Another father said it is too hard for him to punish his son unless he is angry with him. Which father really loved his son should be obvious. The most effective discipline is administered by a loving father who himself suffers with the one being disciplined.

Begin with the infant in training to obey. Perhaps the first training an infant gets in obedience is when he gets his bath. He may cry in protest but his mother goes on and finishes his bath anyway. You say, "That's normal." Yes, it is, and it should be just as natural for the mother two or three years later to see that the child gets to bed at the

58

proper time, even though he cries in protest and refuses to go. To carry this farther, when the child is twelve years of age and is told to wear a coat when he goes out in the cold, it should be understood that he wears a coat.

If the little child is told not to take a small ceramic ornament off the shelf and does so, the mother might need to lead the child back to the shelf, gently take his hand, and make him set it back in its place. If he repeats this forbidden act, he might need a slap on his hand. The slap should give him definite pain. It should not resemble a love pat.

If the child has not learned obedience in his first three years, he will have trouble later. The child should have the experience of learning obedience by force while he is young enough that the memory of the pain will not stay with him. When we see a four or five-year-old making his mother give in to him, we have every reason in the world to pity that child because he is headed for a stormy future.

You need to be strict with your child. Just being strict does not alienate children from their parents. There is no better formula for teaching obedience than a mixture of equal parts of strictness and love. Strictness without love is tyranny. Love without strictness is not genuine love. Tyranny is destructive, and false love will lead to permissiveness, which also destroys.

You have no doubt heard more than one person praise his father for having been strict with him when he was young. You may also have heard dishonoring remarks from people who had easy-going, permissive parents when they were young.

In teaching obedience, don't fail to impress on your child the need to be fully obedient to God's Word, the Bible. This is the highest authority we have. Children are first of all responsible to their parents, then to God, and then to the church. When they become Christians, the order may be changed somewhat. They are then directly responsible to God, but they are also responsible to obey their parents and the church. Then follow other authorities, such as civil officers and schoolteachers. Children should be taught that if any other authority says anything different from what God says, they should obey God rather than man.

Always be reasonable with your child. Children can quickly sense when a command is reasonable. Making unreasonable demands of children undermines the child's confidence in the parent. Children can also sense when a small matter is blown up into a big issue and when a punishment is inappropriate for an offense.

Depending on your neighborhood, your children might be given nearly the same privileges as the neighbor's children have. It is reasonable to children to follow a standard of conduct that is common to the neighborhood. However, when anything about the standards of the neighborhood is sub-Christian, it should be understood that we are to be faithful first of all to God. Children will understand this even though they will be different from their neighbors.

Restrictions that are set for the children should be carefully explained, such as why they are not allowed to go to the movies with the neighbor's children. The reasons should be plainly given to them and the strength of parental authority must be applied to help children refrain from what they know is wrong. Children often know what is right or wrong but do not have the moral strength to do right without some support. That is why children have parents! Be sure to be reasonable, firm, and loving.

Many times parents have lost the opportunity to be helpful to their children because they have not insisted that they obey. Children sometimes argue with their parents even though they know their parents are right. Often children are disappointed when parents do not insist on obedience.

Don't threaten unless you are going to carry it out.

Children are even quicker than grown-ups to sense insincerity in threats as well as in promises. Repeated threats with no corresponding actions soon make the children "hard."

One father told his little boy five or six times each meal that if he didn't behave, he would be penned in the bathroom. The poor boy (he was really to be pitied) was never once penned in the bathroom. This kind of threatening and nagging does definite damage to the child's personality. Such a child will grow up to take a similarly hard attitude toward the Bible and the church. In his mind, it doesn't make much difference whether one obeys or not.

Generally, threatening is useless or worse. If the little boy would have been penned in the bathroom once or twice without advance threatening, he would likely have obeyed after that. To threaten a child before he commits or repeats misconduct is demoralizing to the child. It tells the child that the parent expects him to do wrong and has already planned the punishment. It makes the boy think that his father is against him, and the boy may turn against the father also.

Never argue with the child. It is surprising how soon a child will argue if he is given a chance to do so. When a parent argues with the child, the situation changes from a parent-child relationship to a contest between persons of an equal footing. In such an argument each one will be more convinced in his position than he was before. When anyone argues about anything, he does not usually convince the other party, but grows stronger in his own position because the oftener he states it the harder it will be for him to back down. Arguments between parent and child are an indication that something has "snapped" in their relationship, for arguing between parent and child is abnormal in the right relationship. The parent who argues with the child is thereby informing the child that he is unsure of himself. With argument he weakens his position.

When a child talks back and the parent answers in kind, then you have an argument. Talking back must be strictly forbidden. If a young child talks back, some type of discipline is needed, and a slap on the mouth may be appropriate. Some child psychologists would object to this kind of discipline (as they would to the use of the rod), but the ill effects of permitting back-talk are a great deal worse than even an inappropriate form of discipline would be. When force is used, it is imperative to avoid using it in anger. There must be evidence of parent-love for the child in such times of correction.

If the child asks a fair question or states a related fact that should be considered in any situation where arguments may arise, then the child deserves a hearing and should be given a fair answer. You must always remember that the child is also a person, and can be injured or helped. The parent who wants to be safe in dealing with a child will continually ask God for divine wisdom.

Self-expression is good, but the present American emphasis on permitting free self-expression in children is not producing flattering results. If young children don't learn to be reserved in self-expression, they will be handicapped for life. Here we also say, "Live and let live," while some people will only say, "Live." It is especially necessary for children to know that there are times when they must not talk.

A child's running from his parent when he refuses to obey or fears punishment is another form of argument and indicates that a breach in the parent-child relationship has taken place. A wise parent will not run after the older child. If he does, a contest between two runners will develop and the parent may not always win. The child must be induced to return to the parent, but he must not be allowed to have his way.

Children should learn when they are very young that running away is futile. When a child of one or two years runs away, the parent must somehow bring him back, even if forcibly. A small child who persists in running from his mother should be spanked for it or otherwise punished so he will learn not to run away. If this is done in a consistent way, it will not take very many spankings to stop it.

The important point in the course of disciplining is to never allow the parent-child interaction to be degraded to the level of a contest. The parent must keep his role as being over the child. As the child grows into his teens, this role of the parent should become more the role of a companion, but parent and child are still not on an equal footing, nor are they in contesting roles.

Be an example of obedience to your child. A parent who keeps the money when a clerk has given him too much change, the father who drives over the speed limit, the parent who disobeys the church rule, or the parents who shirk their community responsibilities, cannot expect to see their children grow up to be obedient. One such false move on the part of a parent can undo years of training in a child's life. When a father knowingly disobeys God, the church, or the state, he is proving to his own son that disobedience does not matter.

When I was small, my brothers and I always sat with our father in church. Since we sat on benches for adults, our feet didn't reach the floor. After I had been sitting a while with my feet dangling, I began to swing them back and forth under the seat. This movement relieved the discomfort I felt. Although I made no noise, when my father noticed my swinging feet, he looked at me and shook his head slightly. My feet stopped swinging at once.

Today many folks would say that my father was too strict and exacting with me—that he should have considered my physical discomfort and let me swing my feet. That was seventy years ago, and even now I would defend my father against those critics. What he taught me in such a quiet, unnoticed way is of vastly more value than physical comfort. I learned to be quiet in church. I did not know the word reverence, but I learned reverence in a practical way.

8

Conduct in Church

In the modern confusion of human values, revolution in moral standards and conduct, disregard of the establishment, and abandon to the sensual, the church is in line for its share of damage also. Church attendance and interest are extremely low in many areas. Preaching as an institution is no more appreciated by many.

These are difficult days in which to bring up children to love and respect the church or to be interested in church attendance. However, if this problem is approached with godly fear by consistent parents, it is not an impossible task.

The foundations for love and proper conduct in church are set right at home in family prayer time. The family of two or more gathering in the living room at a regular time each day for a session with God is a church in miniature. This is a necessary and vital phase in the training of a child. The father is the leader—the priest; the mother is the attendant—the deaconess; the children are the laity—the congregation. When family worship is properly conducted, children will grow to be respectful toward the church. Consider these important elements in training children in proper conduct in church.

Early in life the child must be taught what church is. To the infant, church is a place where he is taken and held on a lap for an hour or two. His mother sings with the rest. The infant hears a voice while the minister preaches. He knows nothing as to the meaning of all this but is learning through sounds, sights, attitudes, and maybe a dozen other things we don't even think of as adults. The foundations in the structure of conduct in church are laid while he is hardly aware of it.

Mother, the church is the first place outside the home to which you should take your little baby. It should be a regular weekly occurrence. The youngest person I ever had in my audience was a five-day-old girl. I am sure that this mother made no mistake in bringing her.

To adults, church is a gathering of Christian believers for the purpose of corporate worship. The gathering may be in a costly edifice or in a very simple church building; it may be out under a tree, or in a tent. It is the gathering of God's people for worship. This concept is what we must impart to our children as they grow from infancy to maturity. It is different from school, but similar to family worship at home.

In this chapter, the meaning of church is the gathered group for corporate worship rather than the body of Christ or the total of all Christians over the world.

The church is not a place for mere entertainment or relaxation. The purpose for meeting is infinitely higher than this. In a child's mind, church can become a place for entertainment when mother is unwise in bringing toys or playing with the child in church. Much was mentioned regarding this in the chapter on "Reverence," so it will not be repeated here. Sometimes, unthinking persons seated next to a mother with a child can cause trouble by playing with the child in various ways. When the child is old enough to talk, he should not require much in toys or other entertainment. It should be noted here that sometimes the nursery class in Sunday school is too much of a play time and amounts to mere entertainment. For the nursery class, Bible stories can be the basis of activity. Paper cutouts and pictures to color can be used to convey Bible truths to children to instill the concept that church is a time we think of God and Jesus.

Teenagers do not need movies to attract them to church services. Young people soon learn that when they want entertainment they can find places where the entertainment is better than in church.

The religious yearning in every child can be appealed to more effectively by singing and Bible reading than by aesthetics or entertainment.

Here we meet God in company with others. Once I saw a Hindu father in India take his ten-year-old boy to an idol temple to worship. The temple was a mere mud structure with a thatch roof, perhaps twenty feet long and open at one end, with the idol sitting at the closed end of the long room. The father showed him how to bow his head and fold his hands when he was about twenty paces from the temple. The boy walked in this posture until he came to the idol. Then he stooped and touched the feet of the clay image, made his offering, and returned again by a precise formula. It did the boy no good but to exercise his religious instinct. He was very sincere and very serious, but deluded. He was taught exactly how he should do and he obeyed, but there was no spiritual life there. It was all human and formal.

Christians have a temple also which is all the members of the church together. The church is called the temple of the Holy Spirit. It is your responsibility as a parent to have your child realize that when he goes to church, he is going where God's Spirit is, and that he there worships the true God in a living temple. Nothing short of deep reverence should mark a child's attitude in church.

Here we are quiet and reverent. Misconduct on the part of children and young people in our church services is usually attributable to the way parents have trained (or failed to train) them.

In a certain church service in which many young people from ten to sixteen years of age were seated in the back of the church, there was so much noise during kneeling for prayer that it was hard to hear the one who led in prayer. (This casts a bad reflection on the parents of these young people.) They spent their time visiting and playing instead of praying corporately with the group. This certainly was grieving the Holy Spirit and dishonoring Christ. Such things are "spots" in our "feasts" (Jude 12).

If children are not trained in reverence while they are quite young, real reverence may not be learned at all. Someone might object and say young children don't understand what reverence is all about. This is not a valid reason for laxity. They can learn reverence before they understand all about it.

In some countries, people think they solve the problem of disturbance from the children by leaving them at home or in a nursery. This is not properly fulfilling the parents' obligation to their children. They have not taught them anything by keeping them from church.

In some churches, children are kept in another room with an adult or a teen-ager who tells them stories or entertains them in some way. There is something to be said for teaching children in ways they can understand, and according to their ages. However, in the matter of corporate church worship, there is more to be said for children and parents worshiping together. The story at the beginning of this chapter illustrates one benefit children receive from sitting with their parents.

In our preaching services it is a very good practice for children to sit with their parents as long as the children are at home. When father and son sit together, and mother and daughter, we have an ideal situation for corporate worship. Where younger boys and girls sit in groups with other children, there is often not much true worship. It should be recognized that in services where the groups are separated according to age, the end result is not always unifying or conducive to spiritual development. In a Sunday school where the primary function is teaching, grouping according to age makes teaching more efficient. The family that lives, works, plays, prays, and worships together is almost bound to stay together in the same precious faith and fellowship.

The Church is not primarily a social institution. Nevertheless there is no better place than church to practice true sociability. There we mingle with our neighbors and friends. We will help to comfort anyone who might have felt lonely or forsaken or out of touch with things. It is through the church that many of the best young men find the best young brides.

It is a good practice to visit, socialize, and fellowship for a few minutes before going home after dismissal. Care must be taken that this socializing does not become more important to us than everything else.

It is best that younger children be kept close to their parents in the ten-to-twenty-minute period after dismissal. This is a good time for the father of young children to meet another father with small children. The wise fathers will not only talk to each other but with each other's children.

In too many cases, after church is dismissed, the small children are free to romp about with other children and become very noisy. This way they forget all ideas of any reverence they learned in the church service. For them, church becomes a free-for-all running and yelling time.

By the example and discipline of the parents, children learn as they grow up that church is for corporate worship first of all, and social contacts must be tempered to fit into this pattern.

In church we worship. Of course this is not the only place for worship, but the primary purpose of church is to worship and to learn.

A young child will not know the meaning of the word worship. He will do plenty of worshiping but will not realize what he is doing. Worship is not merely singing, praying, or listening to the Word. In these exercises we meet God. Worship is what happens in the heart when one meets God. Adoration, praise, love, or thankfulness—none of these terms is adequate to define worship, but all are descriptive of it.

Little children often, or perhaps always, worship some other human being, usually an adult. The parents are usually the object of the child's worship. This is only natural. The parent's grand privilege is to lead the child to worship God—to transfer the child's worship of the parent to the worship of God. It is the child's "god" leading the child to worship God.

A tremendous responsibility falls on me when a little boy or girl sitting next to me in church during singing, preaching, or prayer, turns his face up to me and for a long time studies my face. I see him out of the corner of my eye, but I dare not turn to look at him now for fear I might spoil something. I only go on singing or listening to the sermon pretending I do not know the little one is studying me. I pray silently that I might be used of God in that moment to teach the little one something that will help him love God more.

Because of the fact that young children worship adults before they worship God, it is best to have an older person as the kindergarten teacher in Sunday school. I could not, and would not, erase from my memory the mental and spiritual experiences I had while I was in the "chart" class seventy years ago with a white-haired man as my teacher. I remember well how I worshiped the old man, and how my whole nervous system responded when he stopped to talk a few words to me after church was dismissed. Now I know how childish (or childlike) it was for me to worship him then, and I have long since ceased to worship him in favor of my Heavenly Father. But I still continue to thank God for my kindergarten teacher.

Here we learn in the best environment. Learning and worship are not only compatible but necessary complements if either one is to be full. Who hasn't seen a six-year-old in school learning rapidly when he had a teacher he liked (and worshiped).

Sometimes it seems we are smothering healthy young intellects by pampering them with gadgets and gimmicks to motivate and make learning seem like play. Some attention should be given to training children in the rugged hard work and effort necessary to gain knowledge. This requires, of course, strong motivation in children so that they will want to learn. I believe that the best motive to cause a child to work hard to gain knowledge and skill is to give him a taste of the results of learning. Nobody can do this as effectively as the parents. In a truly Christian home, where everyone is loved, and where parents sympathetically respond to make facts interesting to the children, we find the most favorable place and time for the true motivation to learn more of what they have "tasted." All that is needed to make a baby cry for more ice cream is to give him his first taste. Then as he eats he will still want more. When he gets older and parents don't put the good things into his mouth anymore, the child will go to great lengths to procure it, even pay as much as fifteen cents a dip, and walk a mile to get it at that price.

The parent who spends his time criticizing the church for not getting better learning facilities for children is not building anything worthwhile. It is better to train the child to be attentive and to get all he can from the preacher or teacher who may not be too outstanding than to criticize. Parents finding fault with teachers and methods contribute to the present rebellion of young people against their teachers and schools.

As a by-product of our affluence, there is too much pampering, featherbedding, and pitying of the children of our land. The results are seen in the rebellions of today. Hordes of young people are left untrained for hard work and for dealing with privations. They are ready to fight and

71

to destroy, for which men need not be trained. They do this by instinct which is left totally unbridled in the absence of training for hardships.

So, dear young parents, spend your time and effort in training your children to want to learn to work and to gain knowledge. Stop criticizing teachers and church leaders. It makes the difference between building and wrecking.

A young man from Pennsylvania whom I knew as a boy went West years ago and finally settled down in the deep forest of Oregon, living in a shack by himself with no neighbors near. He did some trapping and hunting and once or twice a year made long trips on foot to a town to sell furs and skins of animals he had caught. He very rarely met other people, but it is interesting to know he was willing to walk seven miles every week to get his mail from a rural mail box. His social instinct wanted contact after all.

9

Social Behavior

The social behavior in adults is largely determined by the influences, teachings, and training that they experienced in their formative years. A certain young boy was finicky about his eating habits and was accustomed to having his mother prepare potatoes and other food especially for him. When the family had baked potatoes, she made a portion of mashed potatoes just for him. Because he didn't like salads, she made one portion of something different just for him. She meant to be loving and kind to him. If she could only have seen ahead a little, she would have realized that she was acting neither lovingly nor kindly toward him!

When he grew up, he realized what problems his mother's "kindnesses" had caused him. His wife refused to cater to his special tastes. He had to learn to eat some things he didn't eat until then. This didn't help their relationship as marriage partners and called for some additional adjustments. Fortunately in this case the adjustments were possible because both were true Christians and worked it out with only some inconvenience.

Wise parents can be a major factor in the making of a well-adjusted citizen, co-worker and Christian servant. Following are some pointers that will contribute to this.

Love is the basis of proper social behavior. For particular situations in our contacts with others, we have certain unwritten rules like those of courtesy. These rules are based on love. One of the first things a child must learn in relation to fellow beings is to be loving. This is often hard for a child to understand. His instincts drive him to jealousy and self-preservation, which, for a while, may have their value to the child but must be controlled for his own good and for the sake of others.

The child will learn to love others more readily by the parents' example than by any other way.

A young child must learn to respect the rights of others. A child can be taught this as soon as he is able to talk.

Often young children are left on their own as they play with others of the same age. They will learn to respect the rights of others if there are stronger ones in the group, but the basis will be fear, and the stronger ones will not learn. The fear motive alone is not dependable.

When children are old enough to be aware of others around them, they must be trained to recognize others—not as persons to use, but as persons with whom to share and live.

The younger child should be taught to submit to the older one, and the older one should be taught to be helpful to the younger. Often it is seen that a younger child is favored because he cries more or because the baby is thought of as a family pet. This is not good.

Children should not be allowed to fight for their rights. Likely the majority of teachers or parents today will not gree to this rule, but it should be noted how adults behave today who were allowed to "fight it out" when they were small. It is absurd to teach children to fight for their rights and then try to stop wars when they are grown.

When Jesus was here, He demanded no rights, let alone fighting for them. Where would we be today if He had fought back?

Children should be made aware that God always sees them. They should be helped to develop a good conscience.

A balanced sense of security must be fostered in the child. A child's social behavior is vitally affected by his personal feeling of security or the lack of it. This is true even in adults. A person who feels secure will be less likely to have critical attitudes toward others. It is the person who fears for his own safety who fights. On the other hand, the one who doesn't feel threatened naturally has a better attitude toward others. The sense of security and wholesome respect for others' rights are related.

Another related factor should be noted. Ironically, when parents make it obvious that they are trying hard to be fair to each child, the children will learn selfishness. If the mother tries to be very impartial by dealing out carefully each portion of food and measuring each piece of cake so as not to cheat anyone, then the children will be especially conscious about being treated fairly. This leads to feelings of insecurity and selfish behavior.

The young child can be trained to be out-going toward other children. Basic to the out-going attitude toward others is love and a sense of security. The attitude of interest in other people is one that is usually "caught" from parents who naturally give themselves to others. Happy is the child who is sure of his parents' genuine love and who sees his parents being interested in the good of other people.

One day when our daughter was five or six, she and I with a girl friend of hers were walking down a street in Calcutta. They were both happy and felt free. They wanted to skip down the sidewalk, so I held their hands and skipped with them. I suppose not one of us was conscious of anyone else along the street. We simply enjoyed each other, and skipped until I got tired. I clearly remember my experience with them that day, enjoying both. One was my own daughter, but it is doubtful that any stranger could have deduced from our behavior which was mine and which was not. These girls are still close friends. They are now mothers, very out-going, and interested in other people. Of course this didn't come about by that one little experience

77

in Calcutta, but it was typical of what helped to shape their personalities.

The parent must be able to accept himself if he wants to train his child to love others. We love others easily when we are satisfied with ourselves. The parent must first have confidence in himself before he can truly love his child. The child will then love himself enough to love others too.

Talking out of turn is a real fault in many children today, especially American children. A child must be taught that there is a time to talk and a time to be quiet. True, we must not squelch the child's questions. He must talk and ask and learn, but he must also learn that there are times not to talk.

It often happens that while a mother is talking with a visitor, a little girl will seem to become jealous for attention and will come to get her mother's attention by asking her for something. If the little girl really has something important to ask or say, the visitor will not mind waiting for the child to be heard. The little girl must never be given the feeling that when company is present she doesn't count with her mother. This could be very damaging.

However, when the child is only jealous for attention, she should not be allowed to interrupt a conversation. This situation requires a wise mother. Some allowance must be made for a very young child, but when the child is old enough to understand such things, it is very poor discipline to let her interrupt a conversation in order to say something.

An older child should be taught the courtesy of not interrupting when someone is reading, unless there is a good reason. In many modern homes the radio is turned on for a story or the news, and the family goes about paying no attention to it, but talking to each other as if the radio were not there. This teaches children to disregard others as they are talking.

When a mother is alone with her child and he wants to

talk, the mother should never tell the child to keep quiet because "I don't have time to talk." Children must talk in order to learn. And they must learn if they are to grow up in a normal way.

It is inspiring to see parents and children who are free with each other in talking and communicating. This is necessary for a happy family, and is the best environment in which to teach children not to talk out of turn.

Never tease your child about a friend of the opposite sex. This can be harmful to the child in one or more of several ways. It can be a way to provoke your child to wrath. It may make him prematurely conscious of sex differences. It may embarrass him unduly, or stir up unhealthy curiosity. It is neither the way to win the confidence of your child, nor to keep communication channels open.

I knew a father who teased his daughter about a certain boy while the family was visiting in another home. The poor twelve-year-old girl was so embarrassed that she cried. Such experiences are not easily forgotten, and likely this adversely affected the girl's attitude toward her father.

When a young boy voluntarily talks about his girl friend, the parents should never rebuke him for it. In our American culture it is normal for children to do this. Young children do this because they hear older ones talking about their friends. They do it as imitators, not out of any improper feelings or urges. The parents should not express surprise or amusement over it, but talk casually and normally with the child, realizing nothing unusual happened.

A five-year-old boy came running home one evening from kindergarten and was eager to tell his mother that he now has a new girl friend. (The mother didn't even know he had one before.) "Is that so," she said. "Who is she?" "Judy Smith, she's cute." "Well, how nice," said mother. They kept on talking about it for a few minutes. Soon the little boy was bubbling over, happy and pleased with his little girl friend, and more yet with his mother.

No type of teasing is conducive to proper feelings and relations between parents and children, but when teasing is about things as delicate as the things just mentioned, then it is doubly harmful.

Teen-agers need advice and instruction concerning courtship. There is no one as well suited for this as parents. Parent-child relationships should be such that either the parent or the teen-ager could broach the subject without fear or embarrassment.

Along with physical changes in the bodies of teen-agers, there are also notable changes in mental attitudes and processes. At a certain point the teen-ager becomes aware of becoming an adult and by some complex combination of changes he tends to lose confidence in his parents' judgment and advice. He feels he knows some things now too, and may even feel he knows more than his parents about what he needs or how he should behave.

A teen-ager who has had a normal childhood of confidence in his parents is in far less danger of going wrong than one whose relationship with his parents has been marred by a lack of wisdom on the part of his parents. It is this type of teen-ager who often complains that his parents do not understand him. Teen-agers of the most careful parents may think they are not understood. Sometimes it is true that parents do not understand, but it is just as often true that the teen-ager doesn't understand his parents —often because he doesn't really want to.

For the beginning of courtship a proper parent-child relationship is imperative. The prelude to a safe, loving, pure, and satisfying courtship is a wholesome, warm relationship with parents up to the time of courtship. The same relationship should also be held during the courtship time.

The parent who is merely passive or overly confident about the teen-ager's courtship is making himself useless.

The parents must keep involved. They must care. They must do much praying for their sons and daughters at this time.

Parents' attitudes toward each other and their examples of proper conduct are very important in helping their sons and daughters conduct themselves properly before others. Deep love between the parents will be evidenced by little courtesies and favors. Engaging in physical intimacies before the children beyond what is considered proper in public is very unwise.

Parents should be careful about appearing before the children undressed. Too much freedom and carelessness in this area has confused children about proper behavior. In the same way, conversation between parents must be discreet and pure. More often than parents are aware of it, young people watch for clues in proper conduct as they observe what parents do or say in their presence.

The American system of courtship is filled with subtle dangers for young people. The greatest danger comes from the fact that some young folks embark alone on this important course, with the parents not being consulted. This is in contrast to customs in some cultures where young people themselves have very little to say or decide concerning a marriage partner. In India parents do it all and find the partner for their son or their daughter. We in our land would do well to assume a more prominent role in the matter of helping our young people find mates. This is an area in which people are very sensitive, and great tact and true love must be the basis of all we do for our children.

To repeat, much prayerfulness is essential in this important matter so that parents and children might be so adjusted to each other that the young people will find the guidance they need.

When my brothers and I were small, our parents always took us along to visit a neighbor family. Once when we returned home, my mother discovered that one of us had brought along one of the toys that belonged to the neighbors. My parents took us back to the neighbors and made us return the toy. I will never forget that occasion, although it was more than seventy years ago. I remember it with thankfulness. This was a sure step toward learning self-discipline.

10

Self-Discipline

Animals act by instinct or by command. A young child is much like an animal in the matter of self-control. Discipline is needed to control these instincts or impulses which are not for the ultimate good.

An infant has a built-in mechanism that causes him to throw up to relieve the pressure if his stomach is too full, but a three-year-old will sometimes follow his inclination to eat until he gets too much, and the parent needs to discipline or restrain him.

Some natural instincts are hard to control, and some people never learn self-discipline. Some instincts are so strong that a person cannot control them until he is born again and has God's grace to discipline himself. Some natural instincts are good and useful in life, but even these must be restrained at times.

Training a child in self-discipline must begin early. Some people say, "You can't put an old head on young shoulders." But there is no excuse for refusing to help that young head to mature as the shoulders grow bigger. Self-discipline is not like a mushroom. It does not just appear some bright morning after a good night's sleep.

Some people say, "Experience is the best teacher." The validity of this is doubtful. Some people just don't learn from experience. In these times when our children's minds and personalities are continuously bombarded by all kinds of revolutionary, rebellious, heretical, and skeptical brainwashing, it is doubtful that any one method of teaching can be cited as the best one. A combination of methods and strategies are required if we want to succeed.

We will consider some areas of need for self-discipline, and find some suggestions for helping the child.

A child will naturally fight back in self-defense when he is threatened or hurt. This is a natural instinct that will show up quite early after infancy. It is a good instinct or God would not have given it, but people have perverted it to wrong uses and dangerous extremes. Self-preservation is desirable, but there are right and wrong ways of trying to attain it. The Bible has something to say about this in Luke 17:33. Jesus said, "Whosoever shall seek to save his life shall lose it; and whosoever shall lose his life shall preserve it." Lot's wife simply turned back to look at her old hometown and thus lost her life.

This Scripture tells us that holding on to earthly things and pleasures is not the way to save ourselves. By the parents' example, a child should catch the attitude that the way of saving one's self is to give up some of the things and ambitions that we so often think are necessary for living. The true Christian concept is not to get rid of those who threaten us, but rather to give them something worthwhile. On the other hand, we do not want our children to be passive or cowardly, but to be aggressive in overcoming enemies by doing them good. If Johnny comes home and complains that Jimmy beat him up, speak kindly of Jimmy and tell Johnny, "Tomorrow I will give you a candy bar to give Jimmy." If Johnny doesn't want to give his enemy a candy bar, try persuading him to try it anyway. Show Johnny that if he beats up Jimmy, he will be doing no better than Jimmy.

When our youngest son was in kindergarten, he had a young British teacher whom he liked. One evening, our son came home elated saying, "The teacher said I was the best boy in school." We asked, "Why?" "Because another little boy hit me and I fought him and won." Our boy liked his teacher, but he liked me even more. I talked to him and showed him that people only hit back when they are afraid. I tried to show him that the boy who can take a beating without fighting back is the stronger one, and if you fight back you are not strong. He accepted what I told him and was helped by it.

A child may eat too much because he has not learned self-discipline. The young child must learn to control his eating. He will not learn this at one meal. Patience and persistence will be required. Sometimes, however, children at certain ages will hardly eat at all. Parents need not be too concerned about this. When they are hungry, they will eat. Self-control in eating will hardly be learned by a child before he is old enough to do some reasoning.

Sometimes a child will eat so much of some food that he will be turned against it. If he eats so much pumpkin pie that he becomes sick, he may never again like pumpkin pie. Parents who really love their child can spare him many future inconveniences through careful restraint in childhood.

Some children will pick out one item on their plates, eat it quickly and ask for more. Soon the child will eat more of that one thing than is good for him and will not have a balanced meal.

The false notion of letting a child make his own decision in everything has been very harmful. The way to train a child to be stubborn is to let him have his own way in every detail. Sometimes a child needs help in gathering things together on the plate. He may play with his food instead of eating, but as soon as the mother picks up the spoon to help, the child at once objects and lets it be known that he wants to feed himself. It is then a mistake to drop the spoon and coax the child to feed himself. Of course the child must learn to feed himself, but not at the expense of learning self-control or self-discipline. If the mother lets the child have his own way, he controls the mother, and the mother feeds his stubborn will instead of his hungry body. Such a child will grow up to be stubborn, which is the very opposite of being self-disciplined.

Eating between meals is a habit for some children. A child may need to eat oftener in a day than an adult, but this should be at regular times. To be nibbling at candy and cookies anytime the child feels inclined to do so is not good for his health. When our children were small, we gave them candy because our doctor encouraged it, but it was always understood that they received their candy only after the meal. They knew where it was kept and they seldom failed to remind us to give it to them, but they never asked for it between meals because they knew they wouldn't get it. This was parent-control of the child, not self-control, but it did teach them self-control, for later in life when they were able to get it themselves, they still observed the after-meal rule.

In teaching self-discipline in eating, children must always be told the reasons for rules or restrictions in order to have a basis for discipline. In India we used tea regularly with our meals and often on other occasions. Our rule was one spoonful of sugar to a cup of tea. They knew why, because I had told them of the many Indian people who had diabetes. (I was wrong in my science, for I did not realize that using too much sugar would not cause diabetes.) One of our children became a medical doctor, and one day he and his family were taking breakfast with us. We had tea, and I had an extra large cup. I took a teaspoon and a half of sugar. My son laughed and said, "I thought the rule was only one spoonful." My science may have been wrong, but my son received the training, and that without resentment.

Self-discipline in matters of sex is of utmost importance. There are many things parents can do to make or break a child in this area while the child is quite young—before the sex instinct asserts itself.

Young children need love to be shown in a physical way. The baby or young child needs to be cuddled (not coddled) by his parents. The teen-ager who was deprived of this kind of love when he was a child is often lacking in self-control in social conduct in the presence of the opposite sex. Young developing girls will often be seduced by what seems to be promised affection which they did not enjoy as small children. The girl who experienced the proper kind of love and affection as a child will as a teen-ager feel secure and will be stable enough to discipline herself.

Self-respect and self-discipline are always companions. The teen-ager who was brought up in a home where cleanliness, order, virtue and purpose are not only the rule, but are fostered in the children, will have gained that self-respect which will call for self-discipline in relationships with the opposite sex.

A child brought up under nagging parents fails to attain a sense of adequacy in judging right or wrong. Continuous parental nagging has done untold harm by unfitting children for self-control when they are not with their parents. Seducers will find ready responses from those who are starved for real friendship.

Desire for possession involves another instinct that, if disciplined, can be very useful. The instinct is not in itself wicked. A small child will reveal this instinct when quite young. It is an essential part of human life to possess things, qualities, and abilities. The baby in the high chair or in the play pen must, as soon as possible, be shown that when he is dispossessed of a certain toy, this is not the end of the world for him. A loving mother who can soothe a crying baby when he has lost something is helping that young life to learn to control himself in times of loss.

Selfishness and self-pity are traits of depraved human nature that children inherit from parents. Nothing so curtails the joy of living as selfishness, and nothing is more destructive to self-respect than self-pity. A devoted Christian must work toward complete freedom from both of these. By proper training, a child can be freed from a great deal of selfishness and self-pity. Yet, to be completely free requires the grace of God in a life that is old enough to realize its need. About the best a parent can do for an infant who is crying because he had to give up to someone, is to divert his attention to something else or to show special affection by taking him up and comforting him.

When a child is old enough to understand, the parent can try to reason with him. If he selfishly took the largest apple, mother might appeal to him to leave that one for someone else. If a child is crying because he pities himself, the parent should become firm or even stern in making the child stop crying. If a child is crying because he was punished, the parent may cause damage to the child's emotions by forcing him to stop. But when he is crying from self-pity, his continued crying can do more harm than being forced to stop.

A mother was looking through a pattern catalog one day and her four-year-old boy climbed up on a chair and leaned on the book she was using so that she could not see. I could hardly restrain myself from taking care of that boy for her, but she only acquiesced to her dear little boy until he forgot what he was about and went to something else. Only then did she go back to her catalog. This was a striking example of training a boy to be selfish. Evidently the boy's motive for covering half of the book was to get the mother's attention. She could have told him kindly to move over, and if he didn't respond, a stern command and forced obedience would have been giving him the kind of attention he needed. Some mothers are very "kind" and permissive to their children, but some day those children will grow up and trample over their mothers' hearts.

When an older child comes home from school pitying himself and complaining to his mother of having been mistreated by the teacher or a playmate, the mother is confronted with a clear choice. She can take the child's part, blaming the other party, or explain to the child that followers of Christ forgive people who are unfair to them. She could, however, ask the child what he did that caused the other to mistreat him. If the mother takes the child's part and thinks her boy would never tell a lie, she is indulging in something very dangerous. Never feed self-pity.

Love of ease (laziness) is much more evident in some children than in others. If a child is lazy in everyday life, he will also be too lazy to discipline himself. Troubles are then multiplied. There are probably very few children who are really lazy. What parents call a lazy boy may actually be a sick boy. There may be some diet deficiency or gland trouble. A doctor may be needed, or the child may merely be thwarted, not having found his real interest as yet. Circumstances may have deprived him of something that would interest him.

A child may be a victim of some unfortunate home-life situation which robs him of healthy ambition, and so seem to be lazy. Some children just hate to work at home, but when they live at a neighbor's or friend's house for a time, they willingly work there like the best of children. It is then obvious that something in the home is not normal.

It seems true that there are very few children who are truly lazy. This malady hits people more when they are older. "Idleness is the devil's workshop," someone said. He likes to keep his shop open.

But some children become lazy when they reach the age of eight or ten. Our modern economy is partially responsible since we can buy all the things we need if we have the money. Children can get the money from their parents, and their wants can be satisfied without working for them.

When I was a boy, my brothers and I occasionally wanted potato chips to eat. Our mother suggested we get a few potatoes from the cellar and showed us how to peel them and make thin slices. Then she told us how to take the dish cloth, wipe the top of the coal range clean and lay the slices of potatoes on top of the dry stove until they were brown on one side. Then we turned them over on the other side until they were brown. With the fork we took them off and then we salted them. When they were cool enough, we ate them. How good they were! We enjoyed preparing the chips, and we enjoyed eating them. Who would do it that way now? With a quarter my grandson can run to the service station and get a bag of chips with little effort. And they are not as good as those we made sixty years ago!

When one U.S. Senator was a boy, he asked his father for a top. His father told him to get a spool from his mother, take his pocket knife and a little stick and make one. The boy started to do as he was told and was gone for a little while. He came back and returned the knife to his father. The father wanted to see the top, and the boy said he didn't want a top after all. The father insisted he take the knife again and make the top. When the boy came back with the top, the father praised him for his accomplishment and showed his delight in his son's work by spinning it. That boy was required to finish what he started and learned self-discipline through it. When he arrived in Washington as a senator, he praised his good father who had taught him self-discipline.

There is nothing wrong with punishing a child for laziness, when it is needed.

Curiosity is necessary and normal in every child. Some children have more of it than others. God gave each of us a share of it to use to His glory. On the other hand, the old saying, "Curiosity killed the cat," is more than just an empty joke. All good gifts are at times abused. Self-discipline is needed in this area also. At times curiosity has caused human beings to suffer reverses or even lose their lives.

Satan stirred up curiosity in Eve which caused her to reach for the forbidden thing after God had warned against it. Curiosity leads many to become addicted to narcotics, to become sex-perverts, to become drunkards, and to fall victim to the cigarette curse—lung cancer. Many people have been confused by reading false doctrines or vain philosophies of men because of curiosity. The sale of pornography prospers largely by appealing to the curiosity of young people.

We are not God that we can probe into all kinds of forbidden mysteries and come out unhurt. There are many new things in the world, in the heavens, and under the ocean which men have not yet discovered or explored, and which by God's permission or provision can be investigated. There are some things, however, that for our own good are best left alone.

Curiosity is one of the strongest of human instincts, and training our children to discipline their curiosity is very important. Most people agree that the majority of the presently televised programs are not for our children's good. Only a blind or careless person would not agree to this. The safest plan is to have no television in the house. From several angles this is the right course to take. Children might be told to turn off certain programs, but curiosity is so compelling that doing this would be about like throwing children into a pool and telling them not to get wet. In some situations, curiosity is so strong that the only sure way to save our children is to avoid unnecessary exposure wherever possible. To train a child in self-discipline over curiosity requires parents who first of all control it in their own lives.

To find the proper balance between encouraging curiosity in the learning and growing processes of our children on the one hand, and controlling curiosity to avoid damage to the child on the other, is a large task for young parents. Is it not true that the Word of God, the Holy

Spirit, and our experience are faithful in labeling those things we and our children should not probe into at all? The Bible expressly forbids some things that are poison as well as others that are harmful. Also, some modern innovations not mentioned in the Bible are damaging. These things require not only alert but praying parents.

The roaming instinct can be very dangerous for a young child. One small boy of four walked into a wooded area and lost his way. He was not home when night came so hundreds of men and boys organized a search for him. About two o'clock in the morning they found him deep in the woods asleep on a flat rock. He was not hurt, but if it had been a cold night, he might have frozen to death in that time. Some children who have strayed away from home in this way were never found again.

A proper fear is an effective deterrent to roaming. To live a normal and useful life we all need a certain degree of fear. A very young child seems to have no fears until he experiences pain from falling. Then fear will help him to avoid falling.

Young children can be taught to fear or not to fear when they are small. Our fifteen-month-old son was not afraid of the dark. After we arrived in India, we had to be careful about walking into a dark room at night because of snakes or scorpions. We had to teach our son to be afraid of the dark in order to protect him. Some parents think that children should never be taught to fear, but this is not realistic. Other parents unwisely frighten their children with police or animals or in other ways. This sometimes works great injustice to the child. It is not fair to the police or helpful to the child to make him fear a policeman.

Lack of fear is not the only reason children wander off. Some mothers turn their small children out of the house to play and don't watch them. We came home one afternoon to find in our carport a little girl less than two years old sitting on the floor with our twenty-foot extension ladder lying across her lap. To me it was a frightening sight. She had wandered over to our house and pulled the ladder over, which had been lying on its side against a wall. The little girl was pinned down and couldn't get loose from the ladder. She had stopped crying and fortunately was not physically injured. I did not know where she lived and, being so young, she couldn't tell me. I held the child in my arm and went to the end of our drive. Soon her mother came from across the street and got her baby.

Sometimes a child will not leave his mother. As soon as the mother is out of sight, he will cry and even sometimes panic. This is a result of the mother's helping the child with everything and hindering him from becoming independent. Such a child will not walk off, but is also in need of training in self-discipline.

Children who are left to themselves much of the time are the ones who wander off. Small children must not be allowed to get out of their parent's sight. Then when they are old enough to understand, they will not be as quick to wander off if they have been trained to be obedient. Self-discipline and true obedience are vitally related.

Temper in a child is good. Train him to control it. A person with no temper will not amount to much. The combination of strong temper and strong self-discipline makes for a strong character. A reasonable number of pounds of pressure in a steam boiler will not explode the boiler because the pressure is controlled. While the steam is under control, it will propel a long heavy train smoothly and surely. But if the boiler is not strong enough to hold the pressure, it will blow up and destroy itself.

Temper is a God-given instinct that makes a person care enough to react in one way or another to any act or circumstance that is unpleasant, unfair, unethical, unyielding, or uncomplimentary. He can either assert, protect, or free himself; or he can control or destroy the offending person or thing. A person with a temper will not just take everything "lying down." He will be like a tempered steel spring—you can bend it, but when it is released, it will spring back to its former position. A person with a temper will not be easily influenced by others, and he will know where he stands. He will cling to his purpose, and will not be dissuaded from any duty he has accepted for himself. He will not remain passive when he sees another person being mistreated.

Anger is the sudden expression of temper that is stirred up. It can raise the blood pressure or tense the nerves or muscles. A person in a fit of anger may be abusive in his language or assault the offender or commit murder. One vain man struck his car with a hammer because the motor wouldn't start. Scripture condemns sinning from such anger. "Let all bitterness, and wrath, and anger, and clamour, and evil speaking, be put away from you, with all malice" (Eph. 4:31).

While anger is a sudden outburst, wrath is holding a grudge or a vicious feeling toward another which usually lingers in the heart a long time. In Ephesians 4:26 we are told to not let the sun go down upon our wrath. We must get rid of the feeling before the day is over. For children this seems easy. They can fight fiercely and in a few minutes be very congenial. A child with a temper will become angry very quickly, but an adult will be given more to wrath.

A child in a fit of anger will probably not benefit by being scolded or struck. These may only increase his anger. Any punishment for anger should be administered after the child has calmed down, but he must know what the punishment is for. To illustrate: if a boy in a fit of anger would hit his playmate over the head with a toy, a kind and loving parent should talk to him to make him see the wrong he has done. If punishment is needed, it should be applied only after both the child and parent are composed and calm. It is so easy for a child to feel that a parent is only

94

taking up the fight for the weaker child, especially if he is punished while he is still angry. It will do the offending child more good to see his mother take up the injured child and comfort him. Later she can talk to the offender, leading him to be sorry for his deed.

Temper tantrums are a little different. A child will scream, slam doors, or kick furniture, and do other similar things to impress those around him. If he succeeds in impressing the parent, he will repeat his tantrums again when an occasion arises. One girl, when she couldn't have her way, would bang her head on the floor in a tantrum. Each time she did this, her mother ran for a cushion and put it under her head so she wouldn't get hurt. This continued until the girl was about twelve years old. It is very obvious that in this case the mother was the cause for the continuation of the habit. The girl could have been saved from all those years of self-torture if the mother would have given her a good spanking the first time, instead of bringing her a cushion. Besides the repulsive habit this girl formed, there is no doubt that her future attitudes were influenced by her success as a child to gain attention by this kind of action. She continued to demand her own way or caused a scene.

Parents must remember that they cannot help a child control his temper by being angry themselves when punishing him. When a mother argues with a child or enters a contest of physical strength, she puts herself on a level with the child. In these situations, parents will need to pray to God for grace to do the right thing at the right time.

If a child in a high chair throws his plate on the floor in a tantrum, it is time to punish him rather than "lovingly" retrieve the plate, replace it, and "kindly" ask the child what he wants. Good judgment must be used in punishment since no two children are alike. For one child a stinging slap on the hand will help, but for another it would be more effective to make him do without food for this meal. For another, a stern command would be enough. Some children are so sensitive that they will even faint upon being spanked. Such a child does not need a spanking. But wrong-doing on the child's part should never be overlooked.

A hot temper in a child makes a very difficult problem with which to deal. Complete victory will not come for the child until he is old enough to be accountable, realizes he needs help, and submits himself to the grace of God in regeneration.

Children often go to extremes in having fun until it becomes pure foolishness. This is not helpful to a growing child. Romping and tusseling are good if kept under control, but there is no good reason for foolishness. When boys and girls are five or six, they must learn some self-control in this area also. They do not often see dangers in rough play and can injure each other. One ten-year-old boy, while playing with another boy, threw a dry ear of corn and hit the other boy on the side of the head, causing instant blindness in one eye. The blow had caused the retina to drop and vision was lost.

It is only reasonable that parents should keep a watchful eye on young children "having fun." They will have opportunities to help them learn self-discipline, even in tusseling. One mother, whose children were the same age as our children, kindly rebuked me for trying to quiet our children down a bit when they were too noisy in the room where we were visiting. This may not be the only reason, but I am sorry to say that her children caused her many heartaches as they grew up.

Children can and should learn self-discipline while they are quite young. They will hardly learn it on their own. Parents have the primary responsibility to teach it to them and must do so if they would have them to be well-adjusted and respectable persons.

When a certain mother looked out the window and saw Mrs. Nabor coming to visit, she remarked to her children, "There comes that big gossip again to take up my time!" But when Mrs. Nabor came to the door, the mother gave her a profuse welcome and told her how glad she was to see her. Learning honesty is difficult for a child in such circumstances.

11

Honesty and Truthfulness

In John 8:44 Jesus, in talking about the devil, said, "He is a liar, and the father of it." It was the devil's lies that caused Adam and Eve to be deceived and fall. One of the most diabolical acts of humans is telling the untruth.

There are people who take it for granted that children will tell lies, and they do very little about it. Some of them say that while children are little they should be allowed to lie, fight, and steal to get it out of their system, and when they grow up they will change. This also is one of the devil's big lies. In cases of even the best trained children, some tendency to dishonesty remains with them.

A child must develop a conscience against dishonesty. In India there are some children of non-Christians who have no conscience against stealing but do have a very sensitive conscience against getting caught. Their mothers commend them for bringing home stolen articles without getting caught. If they get caught, mothers punish them. This results in a strong conscience trained the wrong way.

There are some parents who seem to think their children could not tell the untruth. One mother said about her daughter, "I know she wouldn't lie." The daughter had lied and then heard what Mother said. This trained the conscience the wrong way also.

Usually the first sign of an infant's depraved nature is its expression of self-will by outbursts of anger. This is usually followed by some form of deception. The little tot will go to a shelf or coffee table on which are some things he would like to play with but has been forbidden to take. He will stop just in reach of the thing he wants, put out his hand toward it, but look at his mother to see if she is looking or if she will permit. If she isn't looking, he will probably take it. This is acting a lie. The wise mother will say "No, no," and the child will get the help he needs to refrain from taking the object. This is training him to develop a conscience. Some mothers may pretend not to notice while the child is taking a forbidden article and then slap his hand after he takes it. This is unwise and unfair. We must not expect a small child to act on his conscience before he has developed it. Conscience is something that must be developed before it will function.

A boy was told to stay in the yard and not go down to the seashore to play. Later, some boys came down the street and called to the one in the yard, asking him to go with them to the beach. The mother was inside the window peeping through the curtain but keeping herself hidden. The boy went to the gate and put his hand on the latch. He turned and looked at every window. Seeing no one, he opened the gate and darted out. When he came home, his mother began to reprimand him for going down to the beach, telling him she was watching from behind the curtain. The boy looked pitifully into her face and said, "Mother, why didn't you tap on the window and help a fellow out?" You say that his conscience should have kept him from going. But remember, he was just a boy and in the process of developing a conscience. His mother, hiding herself and letting the boy go against orders, let him know that it was not too important to stay home from the beach. What she did was damaging to the boy, and at the same time losing an opportunity to develop his conscience.

Another way to help a child develop his conscience is to teach him to admit wrong, and if there is a need, to apologize to any person he has wronged. There is probably not much gained by a mother's making the child apologize to her. When the child does voluntarily apologize to the parent for a wrong, then the parent must very graciously accept the child's apology.

You as a parent must be very careful not to give your child the impression that what he did was wrong only because you say so. The child should be kept God-conscious and should know that what he did was against God's will. This, of course, applies to a child who is old enough to understand right from wrong. It is a good practice to pray with the child for forgiveness when he has done wrong. This, however, must be done carefully so the child will not be embittered toward prayer.

Differences in conscience among people of various communities or groups cause confusion in children's minds. We have some people who consider it much worse to cheat a friend or a neighbor than to cheat the government or a corporation. In America we think a person has ruined his reputation when he tells a lie, but when he gets angry, we tend to overlook it, thinking that it shows he is made of good stuff. In India the opposite is true. They will easily forgive one for being dishonest but will hardly forget if one gets angry. Our children must be taught honesty on the Christian basis of God's holiness and of love for others. Then human differences in conscience will be less confusing.

Parents teach honesty by example more than by precept. Somebody said, "What you do speaks so loudly I can't hear what you say." It is time we go one step further by changing that saying to, "What you *are* convinces me more than what you say or do." Many parents are not aware that they cannot hide their real selves from their children. A child knows when a parent pretends to be better than he really is. We can be glad that a child also knows when his parents are thoroughly honest. These things very definitely affect children.

A mother did irreparable damage to her daughters when she suddenly said to them, "Girls, put those things away,

Daddy's coming." Those girls cheated their daddy more than just that once. But the worst cheating was done by the mother to the girls.

When a father comes home from the store and says, "The clerk gave me too much change, but I just kept it," he does something which the children will never forget.

Once a well-dressed lady customer in a food market glanced around a bit, dumped three boxes of strawberries on the table, proceeded to pick up the choice berries, and put them in one box. She then put that box into her basket to take with her and put the rest of the berries back into the other two boxes for someone else to buy or leave. She didn't get caught just then, but it is sad to think what her children might have been like if she had any.

Happy is the parent whose children call him honest. But the children are no less happy for having such parents, and furthermore, they are better fitted to live useful lives.

Exaggeration is never consistent with honesty. Certain common expressions border on the questionable, such as, "I was scared to death," "Thanks a million," "Everybody's doing it." It would be interesting to know what thoughts cross a child's mind when he first hears his mother say, "I died laughing." Such statements as these are generally considered to be harmless, but they can have bad effects. The parents' example is most effective in teaching children regarding exaggeration. The kind of exaggeration that is even more improper is when someone catches an eight-inch fish that grows to sixteen inches by the time the neighbors hear about it!

One should not teach a child to be unduly conscientious so that when he is grown he will worry over having said it was ten minutes past two when it was only nine minutes past. But when one is in the habit of exaggerating in things like, "He hit me with a big rock," when it was only a very small pebble, then it is time to do something about it. A child or a childish person usually exaggerates to get

102

attention or sympathy for himself. If your child comes with a story like this, don't act surprised or show sympathy, but start asking questions about the size of the rock until it becomes clear that it was only a pebble. Then talk calmly, but firmly, about the seriousness of telling this type of lie. Instead of letting the child call your attention to his "suffering," you get his attention on his dishonesty. He will try to be more careful after that.

Honesty in school must be insisted upon by parents and teachers. The temptation to cheat in order to pass is real and great for a youngster in school. It is often very easy to get help in a test, which makes it all the more tempting. This is a very common area of dishonesty in children. With so many children cheating, the one who doesn't cheat is sometimes labeled by the others as being odd. It is good to teach our children individuality so they will not hesitate to stand alone for the right. You should never suspect your child of having cheated just because he has a good grade. However, if any evidence comes up that he might have cheated, you should trace it out in a wise way so as not to discourage an innocent child. If your child is found to have cheated, don't act surprised, but be firm in teaching him against cheating and have him go to his teacher and apologize. If it seems too hard for the child to go alone, then one parent should go with him. Don't force a timid child to go alone to apologize, if he is unwilling, but don't overlook the wrong either. Let the child know how important honesty is.

The damage to your child's personality from being called a "square" by other children is not great at all compared to the damage you bring to the child by ignoring real dishonesty in his work or attitude.

God knows everything, and He is the final judge. Your child must know this. It is proper to let the child know that he might deceive you or the teacher, but that God cannot be deceived. A six-year-old can grasp this concept, and it is very important that he thinks of God as the final one to whom he must answer. First of all, the child should know that God loves us, is just and fair, and doesn't want us to do wrong. It fosters a feeling of security when the child learns early that he is worth something, that God loves him, doesn't want him to be dishonest, knows everything, and will punish evil. This is the way a child should be brought up, and every parent should strive to be as nearly like God in this matter as possible.

Another very important part of a child's training in honesty is prayer. Each time an incident comes up, there should be teaching, rebuking, and correcting. But each such session with an erring child should be concluded with prayer. Both the child and the parent should pray audibly.

Do you, young parent, ever feel your great inadequacy to properly train your child? Turn to God in prayer, and you can again go on in confidence.

Making and keeping promises by parents is a very important matter. You must make promises only in sincere honesty. The same honesty must motivate the keeping of your promises. When parents are strictly honest in everything—especially in making and keeping promises—then the child catches the importance of honesty in his behavior also.

If you make a promise, *keep it,* even if the price has gone up. When it becomes impossible to keep a promise, then honestly explain it to your child. In such a case, the parent's honesty cannot be questioned by the child.

Don't make promises unless you are sure that you can keep them. Also, never threaten any punishment without standing by it to the end. Making promises and threats to a child and then not keeping them is very demoralizing; such a child has all the chances to be dishonest as he grows up.

It is always better to make few promises, but when you make a promise, make it for something worthwhile. A promise should never be used to bribe a child to do something he already knows is his duty. Neither is it good to threaten punishments often. Continual threatenings will affect the child's attitude toward the parent adversely. Punishment is not more effective because it follows a threat. It is much better to punish when necessary without first threatening.

The Santa Claus myth is of purely pagan and diabolical origin. It has done no one any good. For Christians, it is inconsistent. Christmas is the time to exalt Christ, but many have obscured the real living Christ with a mythical figure called Santa Claus. Young children believe what their parents tell them, and when they discover they have been deceived, the result can be any one of a number of tragedies. Young children have cried as if they were broken-hearted when they were told that it is all untrue.

As a father of young children, it will be better to have your children conscious that you, not Santa, are keeping the presents hidden until Christmas. In this way, the surprise element is there, and the children are grateful to their parents instead of some non-existent old man. The big thing is that the children are not being deceived this way.

There is another phase of the Santa Claus myth that is very wrong. When children are told that if they are good Santa Claus will give them the presents they want, they are getting perverted teaching. Jesus didn't come to reward the good and ignore the wicked. God sends the rain and sunshine on the righteous and the unrighteous. A good parent will not give presents to some of his children and deprive the others because they have been bad. These human inventions will only result in confusion in children's minds, and are based on pure imagination instead of truth.

You may say you talk to your child about Santa Claus but tell him it is only make-believe. What has been gained by that? A child is influenced for good by a strictly honest parent, but when the child lives on self-imposed or parent-imposed illusions, his life tends to become shallow and artificial, and his natural hunger for reality is not satisfied. One of the evils of our time is too much make-believe. Too many "Christians" are hypocrites.

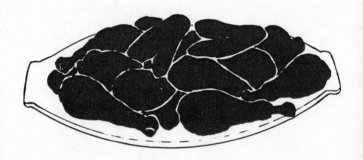

Years ago a young boy who was a neighbor to my wife's family came to their house to visit and play with the children. Before Jimmy left his home in the morning, his mother said to him, "Don't forget your table manners; say, 'No ma'am,' 'Thank you, Sir,' and 'If you please.'"

Nodding to his mother, he ran out the door and down the path toward the Luther home.

Soon it was mealtime, and Jimmy found himself at the large table with his host family. The bread was passed and someone asked him, "Would you like some bread?" "No ma'am, thank you, Sir, and if you please." Poor Jimmy hardly knew why everyone laughed so much, and he was embarrassed. Soon a big plate filled with fried chicken was passed. Father Luther asked Jimmy, "Which piece do you want?" Promply he replied, "Half that please."

The poor boy was in trouble because he was not trained in manners, but was only told a few things at the last minute.

12

Courtesy and Table Manners

There are certain groups in America among whom good manners and courtesy are conspicuously absent. I was acquainted with a group in a certain locality who even felt it was a mark of evil pride to be courteous. Such conditions could be changed in one generation if the parents would properly train their children in this area of behavior.

Parents must be proper examples of courteous living if they would train their children to be courteous. I read an account in a news magazine in India years ago of a young boy who had been kept for a few years by a mother wolf after she found him as an abandoned baby. When he was later found by some workmen in the woods, he was scampering about on all fours with some wolves. He barked like a wolf and bit the people who captured him. When he wanted to get out of a room in the house where they kept him, he scratched at the door until someone opened it for him. He ate his food much as a dog would eat.

It would no doubt surprise us to find how much we learn from our environment and our parents' examples. The mother wolf could not tell the boy how to act and live, but he acted just like she did.

Consistency is a jewel also in the matter of training children in courtesy. We parents must require (and practice) courtesy on every occasion and toward friend and foe. I find it easier to be courteous toward those I consider my superiors than toward those who I think are inferior. This is not right.

I once observed a prominent church leader in Lancaster, Pennsylvania, in a social setting. He happened to be seated next to a man who was mentally handicapped and was only able to think and talk like a young boy. This gracious church leader was just as much at ease with this partner as he would have been with any other. This impressed me so that I never forgot it, and I prayed for grace to be like that.

Sometimes we are very courteous and well-mannered when company comes to our house, but when we are alone with our own family, we forget about courtesy. This is inconsistent and will undercut any teaching in courtesy we might try to give our children.

The basis for courtesy and etiquette is Christian love and consideration for others. Books and manuals on etiquette and good manners may aid in polishing our behavior, but the one true motivation for proper action toward others is love. There are many people who have never read manuals on etiquette but are faultless in their attitudes and actions toward others.

Christian love remains unmatched as the master motive in this. A few years ago I read of an incident during the Congo uprising involving a Miss Hagey from Ohio who was a missionary in the Congo. I was again greatly impressed by what the love of God in one's life can do, even in dealing with enemies.

Some rebel men were herding a group of captives, including Miss Hagey, on a journey to a far-off town. Miss Hagey became exhausted and fell in the grass along the roadside. She had been lying there for a while when a strong evil-looking man came along and saw her. He went to her, bent over her in a threatening posture, and said, "I'll kill you." She said calmly and sincerely, "You may kill me, but I first want to tell you that God loves you." The man changed his mind, helped her along to the next town, and let her join her people again. Her life was saved, and she finally returned to her home in Ohio.

110

If you as young parents teach your children courtesy based on love for others, this kind of incident might be repeated some day in the future. Miss Hagey, too, at one time was a little girl in a young couple's home.

Cultural differences in countries and communities must be taken into account when we train our children. In India it is considered very bad manners to eat anything out of one's left hand. There is a good reason for this in India, but in American culture it is not considered wrong. Also in India it is very much appreciated by the village people if they are asked what they had for breakfast or dinner. In fact, one who is well acquainted with us may feel offended if we do not ask. In America, as you know, the opposite is true.

Similar differences in customs could be cited between communities in America. We must train our children to fit into the circles in which we live. This, however, has limitations when Christian principles are involved.

Being courteous toward all ages, old and young, is essential in right living. In the Bible we have a story of some children mocking a middle-aged man and calling him a bald-head. God himself intervened here and let two bears come out of the woods and maul forty-two children.

The atmosphere, spirit, and rapport of the home should not be the kind that will encourage children to later call their parents "the old man" and "the old woman." It is so easy and natural for young children to respect old age when their parents have the right attitude.

I knew a boy three or four years of age who did not see his grandfather very often but when he did see him he would for no apparent reason walk over to his chair and slap him in the face. This could have been otherwise had the boy's parents been wiser.

Sometimes I observe that when visitors come to homes where there are young children, one of the children will quickly go and occupy the largest and best chair leaving the

111

less comfortable chair for an elderly person. What is worse than that is for the parents not to be concerned about this discourtesy. Or, maybe the father would say he is only treating the boy as a person also having rights. The boy can be made to feel that he is a person in many other ways without undermining his respect for others older than he.

When children are not taught otherwise, they will run through the door first, take the largest apple, occupy the best chair, interrupt when others are talking, and do many other improper things because they are born with perverted instincts and tendencies. It is comparatively easy to train them in higher standards when the parents are willing to exercise wisdom.

I knew of a freshman in one of our church high schools who, early in the term, chanced to meet the president of the school in the dormitory hall. The president was a dignified, loving, and kind Christian man. This thoughtless, rude boy called out loudly as he met the president, "Hi, John!" The president was too good a man to be offended at this, but the boy should have been taught better by his parents. Let us hope that your little Johnny will never do this.

Table manners are very important and they must be taught to the children. I had a very heart-warming experience one time when we visited my wife's brother and his family. At the table, I sat to the right of their son. When the food was passed it was his lot to pass the meat plate and serving dishes to me. The unfeigned courtesy and love with which he passed those things—even turning a little in his chair and using both hands on the dish—was very touching. How could I feel otherwise but welcome at their house and appreciate that here was someone who had been taught good table manners.

In contrast to this, I too often notice that after people help themselves to a portion of food, they set the serving dish down next to their plates with a "plunk," and if I want

112

some, I can just reach over and help myself. These little acts reveal a great deal regarding the thoughts, feelings, and character of the people who do them.

When I was a young boy, I went with my father to town and we got our lunch at a restaurant. At a table across the aisle, a farmer with his two teen-age sons sat eating their lunch. What I saw was ridiculous. They all sat with their elbows spread on the table, each one taking up enough room for two persons, eating fast, taking big mouthfuls, slurping and belching. Altogether it made a "circus" for me as a young boy. I haven't forgotten this yet even though sixty-five years have passed.

I am glad I can name dozens of examples of the right kind of manners, and I thank God there were so many in days past who trained their children in good manners.

Unselfishness is a godly virtue that makes good behavior almost a natural thing for children. This is a key to correct manners.

My mother never allowed us to eat candy or anything else in front of other people who did not have something to eat. Of course, if we could offer them something to eat too, it was all right to eat.

The mother who stops her child from talking in when she and someone else are talking is doing her child a great favor. In contrast, the mother who stops in the middle of her conversation with another person to let her child talk and to listen to the child is doing her child a disservice.

It would be good for parents with their children who can read and write to make a list of little courtesies that would make life more pleasant. Some examples might be: opening the door and holding it open for someone else to walk through; placing the money into the cashier's hand at the check-out instead of throwing it down on the counter; saying, "Thank you," "Good morning," "Pardon me," "Excuse me," and "Please." Such a list can mean a lot to your child. Some people feel awkward in saying "Pardon me" when they tramp on someone's toes, so they just grunt or say "Oops." Absurd!

Christian courtesy makes life go smoothly for the one who practices it and also for the one who receives the courtesies.

When I was a boy, some other boys and I once built a dam, carrying in rocks and sod to build the barrier across the stream. We did it because we enjoyed it. We stuck to it till we had finished even though we were not compelled to do so. People call this play.

Some men in our vicinity were building another dam at that time. It was a bigger one on a bigger river. They were compelled to stick to their work till it was finished. People call this work.

We wanted a dam so we could wade in deeper water. Some parts of our play were really work, but the work was done willingly because we had a goal in mind. We kept on planning, discussing, agreeing, and working until we had finished. This is diligence.

In order to teach your child diligence, you should see to it that he doesn't stop in his project until it is finished. Someone said that building our small dam was of no special importance since it was just play. I don't agree with that. The larger dam was built to supply water to a city, but the smaller dam involved building character in young boys. The building of this little dam had important consequences.

116

13

Diligence

Children can easily get the idea from parents that work is a necessary evil. This would be unfortunate. Work can be rewarding. I like to work, and I dread any prospect of having nothing to do. There are times when some work becomes a bit tiresome or monotonous, but that does not make work undesirable.

There are so many ways in which parents can teach diligence to the child, and there is such a dearth of real diligence among workers today. The least excuse or unpleasantness in work will be adequate cause for many to quit. How sad!

Teaching children to play purposefully and diligently is one of the first essentials in training them to be diligent in other things as they develop. After our granddaughter was thrown off a pony she was riding, she said, "I won't ride him again very soon." Her wise doctor wouldn't hear to that and said, "As soon as you get well, you go right out and ride that pony as if nothing had happened."

If your son can't beat you at checkers, don't purposely make a blunder to let him win. Rather tell him how to play so he can win by himself.

Play is important for a child. In play, children develop character, personality, and usefulness at the same time they are developing muscles, co-ordination, and judgment. We don't philosophize and tell a child that play is good for him, but we must also avoid giving him any idea that play is not legitimate or honorable. He should never be belittled because he likes to play. One shouldn't even tease a boy who likes to play with dolls or call a girl a tomboy when she plays with a hammer. Children and play belong together just like flowers belong to summer.

If your child suddenly quits playing, you should discover the reason. If it is because he didn't succeed in making what he wanted to with his blocks, you should encourage him to try again and even get down on the floor and help. Don't let him give up passively.

Real fulfillment in life does not come in money or wealth.

When our children became old enough to think about a life work, we purposely avoided influencing them to choose a trade or profession on the basis of the financial gain. Let the child choose something he likes to do or is well qualified to do so he will have a natural motivation to be diligent in it. Nothing in life is more satisfying for a Christian than to know that in his work he is helping other people.

To see your son or daughter diligent in the work he or she likes because he can do good to others will be worth more to you than having a luxurious home and children with large bank accounts.

Diligence is not developed by making work seem like play. Let your child play most of the time while he is young. As he gets older, he should have more work along with his play. He should know that work must be done even if it is not always pleasant. I didn't especially enjoy scrubbing the floor when I was young, but I did enjoy scrubbing the floor for my mother. Mother made the difference.

Some parents and teachers think they should make work seem like play so their children will like it. When a teen-ager needs to feel that work is like play, he is not "grown up" enough for his age. By this time he should have the ability to evaluate certain activities and do them for better reasons than just for fun. When children are grown, then the rule should be work with a very minimum of play. Paul said, "When I became a man I put away childish things."

The creative instinct is an important factor in fostering diligence. We are created in the image of God the Creator. Children begin to show this instinct at about two years of age, and it increases as the child matures.

One father who did not fully realize this bought a nicely painted metal toy gas station including gasoline pumps and all. He set the toy on the floor for his boy to play with and left the room for a few minutes. When the kind-hearted father came back, the gas station was lying upside down in the corner of the room, and the boy was busy creating one with some blocks, books, bottles, and other items. The boy wanted to make things for himself.

My youngest brother was about eight when my mother bought him an erector set with which he could make various kinds of buildings and machines as pictured in the book that came with the set. He spent much time with this set and one day came up with a new structure which was not pictured in the book. It was something that showed a good bit of originality. Since the company offered a prize for any original structure made by a boy under ten, I took a photo of his new structure and sent it to the toy company. My brother was rewarded with a new and better erector set, and the next book that came out contained a picture of his new structure. My brother is now a very busy builder of real houses.

Many parents today think they must buy bicycles or motorcycles for their boys. They cost more than erector sets and are not worth nearly as much to a normal boy who needs to learn diligence in working. (This is not saying anything against boys having bicycles.)

The spirit of competition also calls for real diligence. It is good to lead a child to improve on his former attainments. Naturally the urge to do better than before will make him work harder. I remember how I as a boy would occasionally earn a reprimand from my parents which made me hurt all over. The way I worked through this hurt was to decide that I would do better the next time. In those instances I was my own competitor and that was good for me.

Not much of real value is gained by prodding our children to compete against other children. True, they may produce things of higher quality by this, but the Christian implications of putting others down in order to accomplish your own goal is not the healthiest for your child. Let him compete against pests, weeds, handicaps, or anything other than persons.

Sometimes small children are unable to compete with their peers, and we must be there to console them when they lose. A little girl in India was walking along the road eating a piece of bread. I heard her crying bitterly and looked around just in time to see a crow snatch the bread from her hand and fly away with it in his beak. Not being able to fly, she couldn't compete. The only thing I could do was try to console her. This could keep her spirit from being broken.

One, Two . . . .

. . . . .

Nine, Ten . . . .

> *One, two—buckle my shoe;*
> *Three, four—shut the door;*
> *Five, six—pick up sticks;*
> *Seven, eight—lay them straight;*
> *Nine, ten—a big fat hen.*

You can see the order and neatness that went into the writing of this little nursery rhyme. The meter is simple and flows smoothly. The rhyme is perfect—two-shoe, four-door, eight-straight, ten-hen. The story speaks of good order. Buckling a shoe is better than leaving it unbuckled. The door is orderly when shut. The scattered sticks should be picked up and laid straight. A fat hen is in good order any day! This is so different from modern art and poetry. (Not saying the above rhyme is a classic.)

I was taught to say this when I was quite young. It is a very childish and a very homely rhyme, yet I remember the mental images it brought to my mind as a child. There is nothing magic or sacred about this, but the mere ring of the meter and rhyme and the frequent repetition of it made indelible impressions on my mind.

14

Neatness and Order

While I was growing up, I was surrounded by influences that made me love order and neatness. And now I also find that God is a God of order. Thousands of things about the creation show this. The Bible is an orderly arrangment of progressive revelation.

Personal neatness and order also includes cleanliness. The young child learns and imbibes many things just from his environment. His personality is as pliable as soft clay. He adapts readily to whatever touches his life. It is just as easy for him to learn good habits as bad ones while he is young.

One mother in our neighborhood said she purposely delayed changing the baby's diaper so he would get tired of it and next time ask for the "potty." What she was really doing was training the baby to feel comfortable in a "mess." Some children feel comfortable in dirt and disorder, and others feel just the opposite—it all depends on how they are trained.

Some children don't mind having dirty faces until they are told that it is not acceptable to others around them. Mike, a six-year-old, came to school one morning with a very dirty face and dirty hands. It was a cold winter morning in the hills of Pennsylvania. Mike lived in a typical coal town and talked broken English because his parents had just come from Europe to work in the coal mines.

After the bell had rung and the children were all in their seats, I said to Mike, "Did you forget to wash this morning?" He said, "De water was freezed and I couldn't

123

wash." "Then why didn't you get some snow in a basin and melt it on the stove so you could wash?"

The next morning it was cold again, but Mike had washed his face—the front side of it. There was a pronounced black halo all around his face. When school took up, he promptly raised his hand and said, "This morning de water was freezed again, but I washed with snow-water." The other children all laughed when they saw the black halo. He was pleased with himself that he had done what I had told him, but he was not yet aware that it was improper for him to have a dirty face.

When our little three-year-old neighbor comes to our house, I often give her candy. After she eats it, she comes to me holding out her sticky hands; so I go with her to the bathroom to help her wash. She feels uncomfortable with sticky hands. Some children wouldn't mind. I always promptly go and help her to wash. It is a little work for me, but I gladly do it for a child who would much rather be clean.

If that little girl wouldn't care about sticky hands, I would know that her mother allowed her to be dirty and sticky when she was small. I readily acknowledge that now and then there is a child who is an exception to the rule. Some children in spite of consistent teaching seem to like being dirty.

The house in which the child gets his first impressions should be kept in order.

I remember some of my childhood experiences along this line. My mother always kept things in their places. She would never go away unless the house was in order. Things had to be clean and in place before she went to bed. The dishes were always washed after each meal before anything else was done. No, she was not fanatical or extreme—it was just natural with her. A teen-age girl was in our home recently and, after I had asked her to straighten things in the living room, she said, "Why? Is someone coming

124

today?" Children that grow up in a home where things are set in order only when company is coming are not being treated fairly. One important part of good motherhood is being a good housekeeper.

Parents need to be examples of order and neatness. A good formula for making hypocrites out of your children is to clean up only when company comes, pray only in church, be pleasant only when a neighbor comes in, quickly run to put on another dress when you see company coming, etc. If you want to have your children grow up to be whole-souled, honest, friendly and useful, do just the opposite of the above mentioned things. That is, be sure your children can feel just as important as the neighbors. Keep orderly and clean when only they are with you in the house. What the children see every day while they are young is what they will grow up to think is right.

Always have all the toys picked up when play-time is over. Have the children pick them up while you wait to see that they do it. Yes, you can do it more quickly yourself, but what have you gained besides a minute of time? Your children are too precious to deprive them of this benefit.

Eric, our two-year-old neighbor, came with his mother to visit. We gave him some toys to play with. When it was time for them to go home, the mother said once, "Eric, pick up all the toys." He promptly did it. This was beautiful. This child is being trained in relating properly to other people, his conscience is being developed, he will be well-adjusted, and his personality and character are being shaped.

Children must learn to help in keeping the house clean. They should not come in with muddy shoes nor throw paper, candy wrappers, or peanut shells on the floor. They can learn quite young to help wash the dishes. They can learn to keep from touching the window-glass and to help with the dusting.

Parents must also guard against nagging the children

about keeping clean which can provoke children to wrath. However, when children grow up knowing that certain things must be in order, they will also grow up feeling secure.

Sosan, an Indian girl, was home from boarding school for summer vacation. I stopped by her house one day and found the mother washing the dishes while Sosan quietly sat by doing nothing. "Why don't you let Sosan help with the dishes?" Mother replied, "I don't want to make her work when she comes home only once in a year." Sosan smiled then, not realizing that she was being cheated.

The child's bedroom must be kept in order. As soon as your child is old enough, you should let him help you in cleaning up the room and making the bed. Then when he is old enough to do it himself, it should be made clear that it is his duty to keep the room in order. The bedroom is very important in a child's life. It is here that he closes his eyes on the scenes of the day, and while he sleeps, those scenes have a way of impressing the tender mind. There it is also that he opens his eyes to the beginning of a new day. Why should his bedroom cause him to start the day with a depressed feeling? The importance of a well-kept bedroom cannot be over-estimated. When I walk through a dormitory in a boarding school and see the order of the rooms in the morning or the afternoon, I can usually tell what kind of homes these students come from.

Clothes should always be hung in their places, beds made, books in their places and furniture arranged in order. The bedroom should show that someone was there between the time of rising and the time of leaving the room.

Church attendance should be understood as a part of the orderly living of the home. Some parents shun any regimentation at all for their children. This is being unrealistic. There are times for strictly requiring approved conduct, and there are times for freedom of individual choice as well. Too much regimentation is bad, and so is too much freedom. In the home there should be many occasions for freedom, and sometimes for restricted freedom. This provides a good climate for a developing conscience.

There is a place for regimentation in a child's life in the matter of church attendance. The child at times may not want to attend church and sit still because of his own bodily preferences and mental impulses. Nevertheless, he should go regularly to church with his parents. There are various ways to motivate a child to attend church with his parents. He can be induced to go to church at times without his being aware of any pressure being used.

In an orderly home, however, there should be no question in the child's mind about going to church. My parents never had any thought that we boys could decide for ourselves whether or not to go. It was just a part of life for our family—orderly family life. And I never heard them say, "You must go, whether you want to or not." I do remember that from the time I was about eleven years old I wanted to go to church, and I would have objected had I been forbidden to go. If I had objected to going, I am sure my father would have had the last word and I would have gone along anyway.

It is hard now for me to understand a teen-ager who says, "I was forced to go to church against my will, and now I am bitter toward things of the church." The first thing I wonder when I hear this is in what kind of a home he grew up.

A well-adjusted child should feel in his inner sense that going to church is a necessary part of good, orderly life. He should feel out of place in not going. He should never even feel that he is going because he has to go.

When I was a boy, my brothers and I didn't have tricycles and trucks and steam shovels and a number of other things boys have nowadays. One spring day we wanted to raise "tomatoes" like my father who was a truck farmer. We hunted some small boards, got sticks for stakes, used a stone for a hammer, and made some toy hotbeds about two feet long and one foot wide. We didn't know what to use for tomato plants, so we looked around the garden and found some small ragweeds which closely resembled tomato plants, and we planted them in our hotbeds. Having planted them in nice straight rows, we felt we had really done something.

When my father came in from the field and saw what we had done, he was displeased because we had planted weeds. He said we had too many weeds already. I don't think any other boys in our neighborhood had any better fathers than I had, but he misunderstood in the case of our hotbeds. He made us tear them out and quit playing with weeds.

15

Toys and Play

Play and toys and children go together like summer and sunshine and grass. It is just natural for children to play. This helps them to develop other instincts and skills.

Toys can teach, train, and influence the children. My brothers and I often rode horses which were only sticks about five feet long. We would straddle the sticks and ride all around the barnyard. Those horses ran, bucked, kicked and even whinnied. They were real horses to us when we combined the sticks with our physical strength and imaginations. Now I like real horses due, in part, to the fact that I exercised my imagination that way when I was a boy.

Little girls play with dolls and by adding a little imagination they actually love them and cuddle them as though they were real babies. They learn this way.

Once a five-year-old nephew of mine appeared in front of me with a toy pistol and "fired" it at me three or four times in fast succession. I said something to his mother about the bad influence this was having on her child. She didn't think there was anything to my suggestion and said, "It's just in play. That's the way for the boy to get it out of his system." She was mistaken. That is the way to really get it *into* the system.

Too many toys can be bad for children. Some parents do not seem to realize that. Once I went into a home where the living room was so strewn with trucks, blocks, dolls, cars, tricycles, etc., that I had to hunt my way across the room. After lunch this generous young father took me to see the children's room in the basement. This room was so full of toys it made the living room look mild.

Children with too many toys tend to be bored and passive, since there is nothing left for their imaginations. They are unfortunate.

Toys should be simple. A fancy, expensively dressed doll serves well as an ornament or to keep for a souvenir, but a simple "Raggedy Ann" doll will give more real satisfaction as a toy.

Too many toys are products of grown folks' ideas of what a child likes. When my brothers and I were small, my mother would let us use the kitchen chairs and a big blanket to make houses and barns on the kitchen floor. We thoroughly enjoyed our playing with them. More recently I have seen boys and girls who were soon bored though playing with nicely built, painted toy barns or doll houses. It is probably due to the fact that there is nothing left for the imagination. The faculty of imagination is more important to happiness and proper development of a child than most people realize.

It is perfectly normal for a child to want to play. Some parents who do not understand think that children play in order to work off surplus energy. You might as well say that people eat just to get rid of the food they have on hand. God gives the child extra energy so he can play and develop as a person. A puppy doesn't play to get rid of its energy. The play instinct is included in its make-up so that it can develop into a strong fighter and self-defender, which qualities a dog needs to survive.

Since play is a normal activity, one should never belittle a child or cause him to feel embarrassed because of it. The child should never be made to feel that he is playing because "he is not big enough to know better." Of course, when an older child plays instead of coming straight home from school, it is another matter. He should know that there are times for play and times for other things. However, children should not be overworked—each child must have a certain amount of playtime.

Organized games and table games that have rules are important for the child who is older. The free play of a small child should decrease as he grows older. Organized games which involve physical exercise are profitable for growing children also.

Table games are not intended for physical exercise, but they develop mental abilities. These games often help "hard losers" get over their weakness.

Small children must be watched when they engage in free play. They could injure each other or themselves. When they are very young, they need to be made aware of dangers and of their responsibility toward playmates.

Sometimes parents will learn by listening to children play. Two little boys were playing in another room just off the kitchen where their mother was working. The boys had lost a small toy penknife. Their mother listened when one of the boys said to the other, "I am going to ask Jesus where it is." Then both stopped playing while one prayed a short prayer. When he finished the prayer, he said right away, "I know now where it is," and went to a closet and found it just where the Lord told him to look.

Improper kinds of play and games must be avoided. As was mentioned before, play and games influence a child's life, and there are some activities which are wrong. Some people disagree on this point, but I feel I have observed and experienced enough to be sure that some types of play have bad influences on children.

"Cops and Robbers" is one such game. Why should a child's world be colored with this type of activity? I can see nothing which would prove that children who play this game would be deterred from doing similar things after they grow up. It would only make them tolerant toward violence.

When I was a young boy, my grandmother gave me a whole set of toy soldiers that could be lined up for battle. I was too young to know the danger in playing with these things, and I am thankful that after I played with them only two or three days, my mother gently took them away from me and got rid of them, telling me war was wrong.

I have seen boys ten to fifteen years of age daring each other to do certain things that were dangerous, like jumping from high places or taking chances in dangerous acts. This type of free play should never be permitted.

Card-playing should not be found in a Christian home, not only because the game is used in gambling, but the symbols and marks on the cards seem to be related to occult powers and magic. Playing any game that involves throwing dice can get children used to dice so they will later easily learn to gamble.

Some benefits from play should be mentioned also. Note the following:

1. Well-directed play will give the child a sense of law and freedom. Today many people seem to think that law takes away freedom, but actually there can be no freedom where there is no law. Children will unconsciously learn this in their play.

2. They will learn to co-operate with other children.

3. Bodily coordination is quickly and naturally learned in play, especially in playing with toys or blocks.

4. The child's mental and physical powers are exercised in a natural way when he plays, helping him on to maturity.

5. In play, the child's instincts are developed, trained, and controlled.

6. The child learns that idleness brings no pleasures and that life has meaning.

Donny sat in his high chair but wasn't making much progress in eating. He didn't seem to be interested. It had no visible effect on him when his mother told him to eat his potatoes so she picked up the spoon and tried to feed him. To this he objected and grabbed the spoon from his mother, who calmly surrendered to him and looked the other way. After all, she thought, he must learn sometime to do things for himself.

I could see the seeds of tragedy. I saw stubbornness, rebellion, and selfishness in the young child, and a lack of wisdom and firmness in the mother. The ultimate result of such a situation could be disastrous. Mother's intentions may have been to teach him independence, but she was unconsciously training him to be self-willed.

16

Independence and Self-Help

Independence is good, but only up to a certain point. It can easily be abused. Many people in this world are too independent to gracefully accept help when they need it. There are some persons who are too independent to yield themselves to Christ for salvation. Isn't it a part of real life to learn to help ourselves by letting others help us—to become independent by being dependent? No one lives to himself or by himself. The proper kind of independence is a virtue and part of a healthy personality.

A human infant is almost completely dependent. A baby chick is almost independent right away. It will begin to find something to eat as soon as its fuzz is dry. It is just as happy under a warm brooder as under its mother's warm body.

A human infant would die if it did not have an older one to care for it. The animals and the birds are provided with instincts and comparatively greater physical strength. In contrast to animals, an infant should eventually develop into a morally responsible being. Therefore, a child's independence must be taught by a responsible adult to enable him to become a responsible independent adult.

A true mother's concern for her child from the beginning is to see him develop into a person who can more and more take care of himself. Even though a new infant is almost completely dependent, it isn't long before he begins to assert himself. If a child, at a young age, is pushed into independence without proper guidance, he will survive, but the part of him that will survive is his depraved nature.

Christian parents should not have their children playing with toy guns "shooting" each other. Young, tender minds should be directed in lines other than in killing people. Otherwise they will become very antisocial persons.

We as parents are happy when our little ones can feed themselves, dress themselves, bathe themselves, watch the time to get ready for the school bus without being told, and many other things related to living and working. But when they disregard our warnings against some of the dangerous things young people get involved in, they give us great concern. When they begin to disregard driving rules because they think they can make it, then we can know that we likely failed somewhere in training them when they were younger.

At a very young age children should be taught self-help in such things as eating, dressing, and the like. We don't tell a three-year-old how to drive a car, but we do implant in his young mind the attitudes and habits which will help him to live responsibly as a teen-ager.

In training young children, we must keep in mind that no one, young or old, can really be independent enough to disregard his Creator. The Bible tells us not to boast ourselves of tomorrow. The training of our children in the area of responsible independence will need to be continued until they are adults. We as adults are not free of the need to learn, even through a whole life span.

In learning self-help, a child must be allowed to make some mistakes without our being too critical of him. Likewise, when he does well, we need to express our approval or commendation. A child needs guidance in order to make fewer mistakes and in order to give him the sense of security that he so much needs.

Once I was visiting a friend whose two-year-old girl was jumping up and down on a springy davenport, with a sharp table fork in her hand. When I expressed my concern about the child's safety, my friend said, "They must learn sometime." That is true, but when is "sometime," and in what way?

A child should first learn to perform with less dangerous things, then he can later be given freedom with more dangerous ones. Many accidents can be avoided in this way. The child's physical well-being is also important. Wisdom on the part of parents is a real boon to a growing child.

One father became concerned because he no longer heard his three-year-old son playing outside the house where he had been working. He went to investigate and found his little son about three-fourths of the way up a ladder which the father had stood against his two-story house. When the father appeared at the foot of the ladder, the child glanced down at him. The father very wisely said, "Go on up to the top, Johnny." Johnny climbed on up, and by the time he got to the top, his father had caught up with him and was able to bring him safely down the ladder.

Don't judge a child's accomplishments by adult standards. A childish effort and childish success are just as valid and real as the best effort and accomplishment of his father or mother.

We have always practiced daily family worship in our home. This included prayer, and we prayed for various causes and persons. Sometimes either my wife or I led. When I called on one of the young children to lead the prayer, he had a very short prayer and didn't cover the ground we older ones always did. I purposely let his short prayer be the prayer for that time without my praying also after he was finished. I wanted him to know that his prayer was adequate, rather than that we older ones needed to add to it.

The objective in training a child in independence and self-help is to help him be the kind of adult who doesn't need to always lean on some other person for confidence. At the same time he must also be the kind of mature adult who recognizes his complete dependence on God who created him, who sustains him, and who is his Lord and Saviour.

Jesus, who worked along with Joseph, was known by neighbors as the carpenter's son, He was the Son of God, but as a good example to all men, He worked.

The first man who ever lived on this earth was given work to do. No one paid him any wages, and no hours were set for him to be on the job or to quit work. He worked during the day and slept at night. No man made him work, and there was no one he could cheat by doing poor work or wasting time. He didn't need to work to earn money to keep up with any Joneses. He worked in a garden, but there were no weeds to pull. He was a free man and happier because he was working.

17

Work

Some folks think they are kind to their children when they don't make them work. Children who are not given work to do and are not taught to work are the children to be pitied.

In defining work, we think of it as effort with a certain object in mind such as making a living. It always involves effort against obstacles. It is effort motivated by necessities for ourselves or for others. By contrast, play is effort or activity for the purpose of entertainment, recreation, amusement, learning, diversion, or simply for exercise.

Some parents think the child's instinct for playing should be utilized to teach him to work, so that work would seem like play. I believe this is wrong. The child should be taught early that play and work are not the same thing. For a child to play is childlikeness, but for a grown-up to always want to play is childishness. Work is a mark of maturity.

One of the pickers in my father's strawberry patch years ago got work and play confused when he persisted in throwing overripe strawberries at other pickers, making spots on their shirts or dresses. This made him both antisocial and inefficient at berry picking. It marked this teen-ager as being childish.

Regardless of a child's age, when he is supposed to work, he should be taught to work, not play.

The lazy child must be dealt with carefully. Some people say that children are not lazy when they are unwilling to play or work, but that something is wrong with their health. I think this is true in a large number of cases, but I also believe there are some children who are really lazy. When the child is unwilling to do anything, either in working or in playing, then there is something physically or emotionally out of order and a doctor should be consulted. But when a child is lazy, he usually refuses to be active in only *some* things. To illustrate, he may not want to help mother with house chores, but he will often agree to play with other children if it doesn't involve too much effort.

A lazy child will always love ease. If there is an apple tree on the other side of the fence, he will be too lazy to climb over the fence to get an apple but will ask one of the other boys to throw one over to him. If he weren't so lazy, he would climb over the fence with the others and find himself a choice apple. Instead, he'll have to be satisfied with one that another boy gives him. If it is too bad, he will say, "Throw me a good one."

One cause of indolence or laziness in a child is that the child is always given everything he wants without any effort on his part. Some parents give their children toys or privileges even when there is no indication that they want them. This is good once in a while but when it becomes the rule, the children suffer.

The lazy child often lacks motivation. If your little girl wants to have a certain kind of doll, tell her that if she keeps her room in good order for one month and works real hard for Mother, she will receive a doll. Then keep your word. Give her a doll when the month is up, no sooner and no later. While she is keeping her room in good order, praise her for her work, and by the time the month is up she will have learned the benefits of work.

Sometimes a lazy child will respond only to chastening with the rod. Whatever it takes, you must keep him from becoming a lazy adult.

The transition from play to work in a child should not be made in such a way that the child is not aware of a change. He should be conscious of the difference. If your boy doesn't know the difference, you tell him that since he is getting bigger and growing up, he will want to help with the work instead of always playing. He may think that playing is a lot of fun, but tell him you've found that work is also very satisfying. It makes you happy when you have finished a job well. Work is good for all of us. Explain to him that everyone should work to earn his living. We do not expect people to give us everything we need. We must work for these things.

As your child grows, he should realize that his food, clothing, and shelter come by hard work and that he must help in the home while he is young. One reason there is so much complaining and discontent among young adults is that they, as children, were not required to work or to obey and respect their parents.

The transition from play to work in a child's life is not automatic, nor is it always natural. Parents must quietly inspire their children day by day, creating a proper atmosphere for work as they discipline them to obey and to discipline themselves.

Too much work for a young child is not good. "All work and no play makes Jack a dull boy." It is not normal for a young child or even a teen-ager to spend all his time working. Such a child will likely develop a warped personality.

In a well-ordered home each child has his work assignments and schedules. One child may be doing the dishes or some other chore while another one is playing and another is reading a book. The next day the order of activities may be changed. The one who played yesterday will be the one to do the dishes today. The point is to let each one have his time to work and also to play or to read.

As the child grows older, he should use a larger portion of his time working. But too much work for a young child can even be injurious to health. I know a maiden lady who is crippled in her shoulders and back, and those who knew her child-life think that it was caused by carrying heavy buckets of water when she was a child. This lady has a very pleasing personality, but she has never married, likely because she is crippled.

There are fringe benefits from work for those children who are taught to work. For children, these fringe benefits may be more valuable than the primary purpose of work—to produce the necessities of life.

As children learn to work, they will develop in personality. My sympathy goes out to a young bride who doesn't know how to cook a decent meal, or a bridegroom who doesn't know what to do for a livelihood because he hasn't learned to work and manage for himself.

It is healthier physically and mentally for teenagers to engage in some useful work for part of their recreation, rather than only playing in school sports and games. I have nothing against jogging, but if students could do some physically strenuous work, this would be even better.

When our two oldest boys were in school, they decided to do some such work along with their school work. They rented a broiler house and raised several thousand chickens. They worked hard morning and evening. When the birds were marketed and all expenses had been paid, they had only twelve dollars to show for their work. They didn't get rich quick, and I pitied them, but they derived other benefits from their work that cannot be valued in dollars and cents. Strenuous physical work and intensive study may be almost opposites in nature, but they make excellent complements.

Work is God-like, and we are created in His image. "Idleness is the devil's workshop," not God's. God does not call lazy people into His work. When you train your child to work, you are helping him to become what God desires him to be and to fit him for even greater work for God. It is a sacred trust to train a child to work.

Work helps to make life worth living. Those young people who would destroy the present establishment and try to live without working cannot be well-adjusted and happy. Only when we work and produce, can we be happy. That is the way we were created.

Whether or not a person knows the Bible, there is an instinctive feeling that some day we will give an account of our activities. We are told in the New Testament that we will be judged according to our works.

Why not reach for true happiness in this life and the next by engaging in productive work and keeping in right relation with God? When you as a parent live by this ideal, your child will "catch" it from you.

I watched some young Indian girls, ages 4 to 6, playing in a village street. When a pregnant nanny goat whose body was very large and bulgy walked by, one of these little girls remarked to the others, "There is a baby in her stomach." The little girl didn't say it lightly or vulgarly, but just as a matter-of-fact observation. The reaction in the other girls was just as natural as if the first girl had said, "I'm hungry." I was glad these small children could be so natural in talking about that subject.

On the other hand, a six-year-old boy once asked his mother where the little calf in the barn came from. The mother replied, "Oh, it just came flying down from the sky." The boy knew this couldn't be true. This mother meant well. She didn't want to tell him anything that would not be good for him. But she was mistaken, and the boy was deprived of the opportunity to learn a valuable lesson on sex.

18

Sex Knowledge

This short chapter cannot even approach a partial course of sex instruction for children. Rather, it contains a few pointers for young parents that might help them to guide their children on a safe path through a society that is shaken with what is called the sex revolution. It may help the growing children to cope with the perverted and dangerous attitudes toward sex that prevail today.

Answer all of the child's questions honestly. Don't say, "I will tell you later when you get older." Your child is old enough for the answer to any question he asks by his own initiative. You will need to word your answers carefully, remembering that you could have a mental background that is tainted by some wrong influences.

If the child asks where a baby came from, tell him, "From its mother's tummy." "How?" "Well, it grew inside her tummy until it was big enough to breathe for itself and strong enough to cry, then it came out and we say it was born."

When our children began asking questions, I took some time and explained how plants multiply, where baby chicks came from, and how kittens are born, and hinted that God made us like that too. From there on I would let them ask questions, and I answered as they asked them.

We had a dog that was about to have pups. When she became large, the boys asked about it and we explained it. Sometime later they came running excitedly to my study and said they saw a puppy coming out of Tiny! I didn't

145

express any undue surprise, but urged them to go and watch for more. They did and told me after each one was born.

The boys went through this experience without the feeling that they saw something they were not supposed to see or that it was something we should not talk about. After that, it was natural for them to ask questions which I answered in a natural way. When they asked questions which I couldn't answer, I told them I didn't know. They knew I was answering them honestly and trusted me with further questions.

Mother, teach your child yourself. Don't vote for sex to be taught in school. There is absolutely no other person better suited than you to teach your child about sex. Sex education should be a project for both parents. Both need not necessarily be present each time, but each should share in the teaching, and their teaching should be the same.

Some school teachers do not themselves have adequate sex knowledge, and they are not emotionally qualified to teach your child in this area.

However, if your school does have sex instruction in the curriculum, see to it that you have the first chance with your child. Teach him before he starts to school. Don't teach him everything you know about sex and sexual behavior, but let his questions be your guide. One teen-age girl's mother told her everything about sex before she was of school age or was emotionally prepared for it. This girl had problems relating to other children and still has certain emotional abnormalities stemming in part from that premature instruction.

Avoid the atmosphere or mysticism about sex. Never tell your child, "You are not old enough to ask such questions." That will make matters all the worse. And if you tell your child anything about the subject, don't tell him not to tell anybody else. This will cause him to assume an abnormal or unnatural attitude toward sex. On a subject as

146

closely related to your child as sex, he has the right to have an honest answer to every question he might ask. Don't give him the impression that he shouldn't ask questions.

Never joke about any aspect of sex. When you help your child in taking his bath (or any other time), don't make light or semi-vulgar remarks about the sex organs. Never tease your child about a girl friend or a boy friend. And never tell off-color jokes about marriage or married couples. These things lead to perverted attitudes toward sex.

Never purposely expose your child to a nude person of the opposite sex. The results could be emotionally harmful. However, if your young son sees you changing his sister's diaper, don't tell him to go away. This is only a natural situation, and if he asks questions, answer them. The same applies when a small girl discovers her baby brother's body as being different. Let this happen when they are young, but do not purposely expose them.

Parents should never engage in such intimacies as petting and fondling in the presence of their children. It is good for parents to express mutual affection between themselves by hugging and kissing. And there is something to be gained by children observing this when done discreetly. But children beyond the infancy stage should by all means sleep in a bedroom separate from their parents. Certainly children should not be given certain sex information before they are mentally or emotionally ready for it, and also there is a wide difference between talking about the sex act and actually seeing it.

Television hinders in proper training of your child. Many concerned people testify to the large amount of violence and sex perversion shown on television. It has already become a telling factor in our present increase of crime. You keep your dangerous medicine bottles out of reach of your child for his physical safety. Why let him have access to the psychical poison by way of television? A child absorbs and is influenced by what he sees much more than by what he hears. In television he both hears and sees.

That baby God has given to you has a right to hear and see in you as parents the things that make for an ideal life, and to experience the influences that will make him a wonderful personality. That is just what you also want.

The sacredness of sex and procreation should be impressed upon the child's mind. God made Adam and Eve male and female so they could love each other and come together in bodily union, each of them contributing a part of himself to a new life God wanted to create in the body of Eve. God created a new life and lets us help Him in the creation act! How wonderful and glorious is this privilege!

It is a noble concept for a growing child to learn that he has a body God wants to use in His work of procreation, as well as a spirit and personality God wants to use in the work of re-creation—giving the good news of salvation so that men and women might be made new creatures in Christ. Both are needed for the population of the earth and of heaven. This is what it is all about.

These noble concepts are being given to your child when he is exposed to the proper atmosphere, parental attitudes and behavior, conversation, and literature in your home. Bible teaching and Biblical living are the best sources for this.

One day years ago in Bihar, India, our oldest son was standing on the bank of a swollen, turbulent river watching several Indian women wading the deep water trying to cross to the other side. Suddenly, one of the women lost her footing and tumbled about in the water. She couldn't regain her footing, and Paul saw she would drown if no one helped her. He had to make a quick decision. He could have reasoned, "I don't know her," or "If I go in to help her and drown myself, what of my family, friends, and work?" But he went at once to help the drowning woman and brought her safely to shore. A wise, quick decision saved a life.

150

19

Decision Making

Life demands making one decision after another. Some people take too much time to decide, and opportunities pass. Others decide blindly without weighing the alternatives. Still others decide on the basis of self-interest or popular sentiment. Some want other people to decide for them. Some avoid situations which call for decisions. Often the most intelligent people have the greatest problem in making decisions. They see more possibilities, involvements, and alternatives and may, therefore, find it harder to decide. If your child learns to make right decisions promptly, he will have an asset in life that can make the difference between success and failure.

Parents must decide for a young child in most situations. As soon as he is old enough, he should be helped in making his own decisions in small matters and even to make decisions himself when his parents are not present. When making major decisions, he should be subject to his parents until he is 18 or 21. The wise parent will help his teen-age children make all major decisions, such as school courses, jobs, dating, and other major projects or activities.

Many children at the age of two will decide small matters for themselves and get into trouble through wrong decisions. Watchful parents will intercept and help the child change his mind. At about three years of age a child can understand, and one can try to reason with him. When he can't reason, he will need to be forced to do what is right. There are mild and harsh ways of forcing a young child to do right, but don't be afraid of the word "force" for a young child.

Don't be afraid to break a child's will. If you don't do it when he is young, he will become a teen-ager who will break your heart. There is a vast difference between breaking a child's will and breaking his spirit. A child's spirit must never be crushed. When a child's will must be crossed, you must always prove your love and concern for him or you may lose his confidence. I don't mean by this that you must give him a candy bar or promise him some kind of peace-offering. Your total attitude toward him while you are correcting him must be one of love.

In our Indian mission at Dhamtari we operated a boy's orphanage. A good warm-hearted Christian man was in charge of the orphanage for some years. After the death of the manager, Jacob Burkhart, when I was conversing with Mukut, who was now a minister and had been one of the boys in the orphanage under "Papa" Burkhart's management, he told me how the boys loved Papa Burkhart although he was very strict, and a number of boys had gotten "canings" from him. Tears came to Mukut's eyes as he continued, "He never whipped any of us without also sitting down and talking it over for a long time." The boys knew he loved them, and that love was mutual.

Your child should learn to weigh factors and choose priorities. Suppose your twelve-year-old boy must decide on accepting an invitation to go with a group to see the Natural Bridge, or to stay at home on a day when an important event is planned in your home town. You should advise your boy to pray for guidance in deciding. You should later discuss the matter with him, help him to think of the factors involved, and help him to see for himself which choice would be best for him. Then let him make his own decision. I believe that when we pray for guidance, the Holy Spirit will guide our reasoning to be in line with God's will.

Your child should know that he belongs to God. All decisions should be made in the light of that fact. It is good to teach a young child that he should live in line with God's will. This is not robbing him of his own will. Having decided to live by God's will, he should be firm and not let anyone persuade him differently.

Some children have strong wills of their own and insist on their own way. Such children become misfits in society if they are not corrected.

The child gets his first impressions about God from his parents. A very young child should be trained to be subject to his parents' will. This attitude will later be transferred as his attitude toward God.

Unselfishness is necessary in a person who would make right decisions. This must be taught to your child as soon as he can learn such things. This doesn't mean a passive, wishy-washy attitude, but a purposeful living for others. Your child can be taught this while he is playing with other children. Here also, the most effective elements in training a child to make decisions with other people's good in mind is the example of the parent.

Honesty is another quality of character you must instill into your child to help him make proper decisions. The Bible tells us that the human heart is very deceitful and wicked. To make decisions that are for your own pleasure or good is easy and human. Young children are usually honest and decide in their own favor since they are naturally selfish. It is when they are older and know they should be unselfish that the human heart makes them believe they are being unselfish although the opposite is true. Honesty with one's self is so difficult that complete honesty is rare.

The Bible raises the question as to who can know his own heart. This is one of the most difficult parts of training a child—to help him to know himself. To be truly honest in judging one's self requires a regenerated mind—a new birth.

Prepare your child for the most important decision of his life, the decision to yield himself to Christ. You, the

153

parent, are the best fitted person to lead your child to this decision. His pastor or Sunday-school teacher can hold only second place to you. You are with your child day and night. Your consistent life and warm love for him will build confidence toward you. You daily try to train him in right living, keep careful watch on his development and pray daily for Holy Spirit guidance. You will then know when to say the right word to help him decide for Christ.

Don't frighten your young child by telling him about hell and judgment. He must be taught about these things, but it is wrong to frighten a young child into confessing Christ. I know by experience the joy that comes when your son or daughter comes to you some day voluntarily expressing his desire to be a Christian.

In the early 20's, when Hershey bars were twice as thick as they are now and cost only a nickel, Julia came to school every morning with a large paper bag of assorted candy and chewing gum. She was the ten-year-old daughter in a family who had recently come from Europe, and her father was earning five dollars a day in a coal mine. I was her teacher, and she told me her father gave her seventy-five cents every morning to spend at the store for candy and gum. She gave most of it away in school as she couldn't have eaten all of it herself and kept her health. She was a pretty girl and had a very pleasing personality, which likely induced her father to be generous toward her with money.

This illustrates the opposite of thrift. Her parents often couldn't make the money reach to the next payday. At that time five dollars a day could have kept two families.

20

Thrift

Thrift involves hard work, controlled spending, regular saving, and gradually improved living standards up to a certain point. I am by no means advocating materialism as a way of life, neither do I say that Christians should hoard their wealth. I do know, however, that the teaching of the Bible makes it clear we are stewards of the things God gives us, and God does not approve our wasting of goods.

Our children should by all means be taught thrift in the true sense. With this they should be trained in giving and in helping others in our present needy world.

Begin to teach your child a right sense of the value of money when he is young. To a very young child, money doesn't mean anything, except that a nice coin might strike his fancy as a toy. A little later he will learn that that coin can be exchanged for some candy, but he still doesn't know that the coin represents work someone has done. The coin for him becomes a sort of magic wand that one uses to get "goodies." Since someone has given him that coin, he will probably edge up to him again for another one when he gets hungry for candy.

Even some grown-ups (in stature, that is) think of money as a magical power to get what they want, and so they try to get money in any way possible, even by cheating, gambling, or robbing. Some people who are considered respectable citizens demand more money for an hour's work than is necessary or fair.

As soon as possible, you should teach your child that someone had to work for the money he has received and it is unfair to expect him to hand it over, unless, of course, he wants to give it as a gift. The child should understand that money should first be used to buy necessary items, such as food or clothes, rather than "goodies" or luxuries. In this way the child will learn that a dollar spent for necessities is better spent and of more real value than a dollar spent for something we really do not need. If one has a proper sense of the value of a dollar, he will be careful how he spends it. This is especially true when one has respect or regard for the person who earned it. In your child's case, it is his respect for you.

After the child is old enough to do some work or run errands—perhaps deliver papers—he should have this opportunity to earn some money. I do not deem it wise to pay a child money for chores or other work at home. Rather, he should have a project of his own. If he would like a bicycle, tell him he can work and save until he can buy a bicycle. Help him to see this and encourage him. After he has bought the bicycle, he will value it much more than if you had just given it to him. He will also take better care of it because he knows how he got it. Dear reader, this is a very important item in these days of general wealth and lack of self-discipline.

Having a purpose in life is essential for the enjoyment, health, and maturing of a growing child. Teen-agers who wonder why they are here are not so much to blame for their condition as are their elders. If they had had the proper home teaching and environment, they would be very different from what they are. Dear young parents, you can save the next generation from purposelessness and aimlessness by training, caring for, and loving them while they are in your custody. If they have no purpose in life, they will be like a ship without a rudder. Their sea will be rough for sailing as present trends indicate.

Your infant has every right to sense that without him your lives would not be full. As he grows and begins to understand what you say, your whole attitude and words to him should be consistent as you tell him, "What would I do without you?" The mother who told her daughter that she was an accident, which amounted to telling her she was not wanted, did her daughter a great injustice. This daughter was accepted into another home at the age of 18 and loved by her new "parents." Although she was emotionally unsettled, there she found stability and was converted to Christian faith. But not all such children will be as fortunate as she was.

Your teen-age child should know what God expects of him and why he is here. By now he should know that the world needs him. If you teach him the precepts of the Bible by word and by example, he will have this consciousness.

The desire to give rather than to get is at the core of a happy life. When a person is born again and yielded to Christ, the love of God is put into his heart, and it becomes natural for him to want to give what he has and what he is for the good of others. But this can be taught to your little one before he is old enough to realize his need of the Savior. Happy is the young person who has been so taught from infancy.

I am convinced that our children have had that kind of spirit from early childhood because they saw every day how their mother literally lived for others. Her motto was "others" even though she never claimed to have any motto. When they wanted her to read to them, she laid aside her own book and did as they requested. This was not only once in a week, it was every day. When they played with their little express wagon, we saw to it that they would give their playmates rides, instead of having it the other way around all the time.

Once, while teaching in a public school, I asked the third grade pupils to write an essay on the subject, "What I Would Do If I Had One Hundred Dollars." The variety of essays was very interesting. Some of the boys wanted to buy a Ford (this was before the days of paying by installment), and if they had any money left, they would make other purchases. One girl named Edith, who came from a poor home, wrote a remarkable essay so different from the others. First, she said she would purchase some necessary items of clothing including shoes and a new dress for her mother because she needed them. Then she wanted to buy her brothers new shoes and sweaters, and if there was any money left, she would buy a pair of gloves for herself. I well knew this girl's lack of good winter clothes, and her essay said much. I wish every home would train children in this way. We would then have more young people with purpose in life in the coming generation.

I have mentioned the foregoing qualities and traits under the heading of this chapter because true thrift does not mean living like a miser but using God-given abilities to increase one's possessions so as to have more to give to others. It also involves purposefulness of life. No one should lay up a fortune for its own sake. What a shallow purpose this would be!

Don't spoil your child by making him accustomed to the choicest foods, the best clothes, and the finest houses. The happiest people in the world have likely never been accustomed to these things. Maybe you will say, "What is wrong with having the best things when we can afford them?" I would say, "Is it right when there are millions who can't even eat once every day?" If you as parents have found that there are better things to enjoy than all the sweets you can eat, then your child will catch the spirit too.

This idea is well expressed in the little proverb coined by a good brother in the church years ago: "Get all you can, can all you get, and give all you can." Your children should learn by experience that there is more enjoyment in giving than in getting. This they will learn more easily when they are old enough to understand, but very young children can learn this too. A three-year-old gift-wrapped her two small

160

toys with her mother's help for her daddy's birthday gift. She undoubtedly enjoyed that as much as an older person would have enjoyed giving some new expensive gift.

Your child can learn thrift with his toys. As was said before, money itself doesn't mean much to your child. But toys do mean a great deal to him, and you must teach him to care for his toys. He should pick them up and put them in their places when he has finished playing. You can help him repair toys that are broken. Don't let him throw away any toy that can be salvaged at all.

I have, in a few instances, found tablespoons, dippers, and other kitchen utensils out in my neighbors' sandboxes, where the children took them to play and never returned them. This is the natural way for children to act, but you must train your child to return things he takes out to play with. Moreover, silverware and cooking utensils are not toys and should not be used as toys.

You might do well to buy your child a small beach bucket and shovel to play with and explain to him why he shouldn't take things out of the kitchen to use as toys. If you cannot afford to buy him a toy bucket and shovel, you can whittle a shovel out of a small piece of board and give him an empty fruit juice can. Improvised toys help children in various ways. Besides being a way to train them in economy and thrift, they encourage originality.

Thrift doesn't necessarily imply being rich. It is not the possession of money that makes a full life. The happiest person is the one who knows how to produce and save, and instead of hoarding things, gives them for the good of others.

"Mamma! Today the teacher told me I was the best boy
in school!" David couldn't run fast enough as he darted
home from school in Darjeeling, India to the cottage where
his mother was making supper.

"Why did your teacher say that?"

"Billy and I were fighting and I won the fight. Miss B.
told me I am the best boy in school."

David was only six and to him it made little difference
whether he beat up another boy or shared his lunch with
him, just so he got his teacher's approval. If David had been
sixteen and had beaten up his classmate, he would have been
accountable to God for his immoral act. At that age he
would have sensed more clearly that he did wrong, and to
beat up a classmate should have troubled his conscience. But
in his innocence, he was led to believe that he had done
right when he had actually done wrong.

21

Sense of Morality

A Christian definition for morality is "proper, virtuous conduct that will always be respectful to self, other people, and God." A baby is innocent, though he sometimes does things or misbehaves in ways which would be considered immoral in older persons. We train small children in proper conduct and right habits so they may be fitted to live virtuously and morally when they are older.

Training your child for moral living must begin in infancy. This begins with training the child to be regular with his sleeping, eating, and other bodily functions. All the things that are so much a part of a child's life should be done at regular times as much as possible. This is not only good for physical health, but it becomes a solid basis for the development of a sound moral character.

A person who has learned to be habitually regular is not necessarily more moral, but habits of regularity make it easier for him to be moral when he becomes older. To instill habits of regularity in a child is to add something to his life which will make for stability.

Train your child to act like a moral person, even though he is not aware of what is moral and what is not. As soon as the infant notices effects of his acts on himself or on others, even though he doesn't know whether these acts are right or wrong, you should be alert and ready to reward him for what you consider good acts on his part. You might reward him with a love pat, by stroking his head with a light hand, or with a smile. Or when he is old enough to understand, you could commend him by saying, "That was nice," or "You are a good boy," or you might give him something he would enjoy having.

When he does things which are wrong, withhold approval or punish when necessary. This way he will discover what meets your approval, and doing right will become a habit. When he reaches the age of understanding, he will more readily develop a sense of morality. A parent's approval or disapproval is a powerful influence. An Indian boy thought it was good to steal, but wrong to get caught, since his mother commended him when he brought stolen things home, but punished him because he got caught whenever this happened.

Self-control is also an important factor in moral behavior.

When your child cries because he gets hurt or is mistreated, give him some assuring words to let him know you care and try to get him to stop crying. For a child to thus stop crying shows genuine self-control. However, if a child cries bitterly because you have just punished him, then never force him or command him to stop crying. After he has had some time to cry, kindly tell him he has cried long enough and that he should now stop. If he can stop only for a while, he will have practiced self-control. He may cry again later, and the same process can be repeated.

If another child hurts him in some way and he wants to retaliate, you should try to persuade him against it. This takes real self-control, but by doing this he will grow. This will equip him with self-control which is essential for moral behavior and which will help him when he is old enough to know right from wrong.

Teach the child that it pays to wait for the things he will enjoy. He may come in before mealtime asking for a piece of the cake you just baked. You as a wise mother will say, "If you want your cake now, you can't have another piece when the rest of us will have cake with ice cream." Try to

164

help him realize why he should wait. If he still insists, then give him a piece, but keep your word and give him none when the family has cake for dessert. Do this while he is young. Waiting in itself is not a moral act. But the ability to wait fits one to live morally.

Jesus told us not to avenge ourselves and that He will repay. If someone strikes me and I have learned to wait, it will be easier for me not to strike back. Remember that you have the opportunity to train your child in patience in his early years so he will be better equipped to live morally throughout his life.

Some parents are permissive with their little children because, as they say, they don't understand. The training must be done even though they don't understand. Do we older ones understand everything we learn?

A good motto for your child is: "Leave the best till last." Work, then play. Meat and potatoes first, then pie. Potatoes will taste better because you anticipate pie afterward. If you eat your pie first, potatoes won't taste nearly so good later. Lessons first, then a sled ride.

There is nothing moral or immoral about when you eat pie. But doesn't waiting for the best often make the difference between moral and immoral acts? It is certainly much better to wait until you have earned money and then buy what you want than get it at once by stealing and afterwards pay for it by sitting in jail. If your child learns while he is small that it is better to first endure pain and then to enjoy pleasure, he has learned a basic principle in overcoming temptation to commit an immoral act.

As far back as I can recall, it was always my habit to do the worst jobs first and leave the more pleasant ones for last. In doing my homework as a school boy, I always first studied the subjects I disliked most, and left my better subjects for last. While I studied history—which was my hardest—I was urged on to my math, which I liked the most. While I was working at my math, my memory of having finished my history made the math all the more pleasant. I also enjoy working or eating this way.

If your child has acquired good habits early, he has a greater advantage as he faces life. You should always insist on right actions. Always appeal to the highest motive that will work.

If a two-year-old insists on taking the ceramic ornament from its place on the shelf or table, you know it is useless to tell him that it is too expensive to use as a toy, that it is improper to play with it, or that he might break it. Look at him and shake your head in disapproval. If that doesn't work, say a firm "No." If that fails to bring a response, slap his hand. Always insist on obedience.

As the child gets older, keep appealing to higher motives. Moral behavior based on low motives isn't worth very much. It might not even be true morality. Along with this training, your love for your child must be made known to him. This will strengthen any method you might use in persuading him to right actions.

A mother who had failed her daughter when she was young, couldn't gain the proper obedience and respect from her. When the girl was in her middle teens, the mother was deeply concerned that she wasn't being obedient. On a few occasions the mother used a paddle on her teen-age daughter. This kind of motivation should have been used when she was a little girl. It was too late when she was sixteen. By this time she should have responded to some higher motivation. The principal effect of the beating now was a deep humiliation and a worsening of the already strained relationship between the two.

The age of moral consciousness in a child usually comes at about twelve years. This corresponds with the age of accountability, the term used by church leaders and evangelists. Some children come to this stage in their development much earlier and some much later. A child in his innocency who strikes his mother is acting by instinct,

166

and although the act may be done in innocence, it must be curbed. After that, the child is no longer totally innocent on that point. He now comes to know how such acts affect himself and others. Furthermore, he is violating God's will and this makes it immoral.

If he is allowed to commit ungodly acts in his innocency, he is being led into immorality as he comes to accountability. If you disallow him to strike you while he is young, he is being prepared for moral behavior as he comes to moral consciousness.

Proper training from infancy is essential and beneficial. This, however, is not enough to insure good moral character. People often violate laws of morality in spite of their training.

Now comes the time to think on another human factor. We are all born with the old Adamic nature which tends to do wrong. The tendency to sin and evil is strong in every human. There is no power within ourselves to live rightly. An unregenerate person does not have the power to live right in the sight of God, even though many unconverted people seem to live clean and moral lives. This only shows what training and right habits can do. This is all good, but it still is not enough.

When your child reaches the age of accountability, he needs to realize his needs and be led to surrender his life to Christ. The work of the Holy Spirit in his heart will generate a new life, and he is then said to be born again by a miracle of God's power. Now he is given the desire and the power to decide the right course when temptations come to him. He will also have the power of the Holy Spirit in his life to enable him to live above evil.

This is the goal of every Christian parent for his child. It is not enough to live a good moral life. He needs to be converted and to be made a new creature in Christ.

The grass in the Indian jungle was about six feet tall, though not very dense. While his father was cutting wood and stacking it up for the government to haul out and sell, little Mohan was playing with his bow and arrow. His father was expert with a giant-size bow and arrow with a long steel arrowhead that killed many wild animals. Father's weapon was lying on the ground just beside the stack of wood he was slowly building. Father wanted Mohan to learn the use of a bow and arrow, so he had given him the boy-size bow and an arrow with a small wooden ball instead of a sharp, pointed tip. This was for safety for Mohan and everyone around him.

In his own way, this practical father taught Mohan the principle of being responsible. Mohan didn't have very many things, but he did know what each thing was for and how and when to use it for good.

Since the father was busily chopping and stacking wood, he did not see the tiger a short distance behind him, cautiously creeping closer and closer. Young Mohan saw the tiger approaching, but being very wise in the ways of the jungle he stood still and said nothing to his father. If he had, the result might easily have been tragic. The tiger had his eye on the working man and came closer by the second, not seeing Mohan, standing quietly in the grass alert to every movement of the beast.

Just as the tiger was about to leap toward his father, Mohan shot his ball-tipped arrow which passed by just in front of the tiger's nose. This frightened and confused the tiger. The tiger made a sharp turn away from the father and ran back into the forest. This is a real picture of a very responsible act by a young boy ten years of age.

22

Sense of Responsibility

I was camping near the place when this occurred. A day or two after this boy's brave deed, I heard of it from a neighbor. The head forest officer also happened through the area and stopped at my camp for a short visit. I told him about this young boy's deed and suggested that he arrange to meet him and give him a reward of some money. The officer was pleased at my suggestion and told me he would surely do this.

A child must be trained to be responsible from infancy. A large share of the training of a child must begin in the first year.

You might say, "What does an infant know about responsibility?" I would answer that he knows nothing. But you must do what you can to shape the pliable little personality so he will grow to be a responsible person.

When your child cries from the discomfort of a wet diaper, be sure to change the diaper as soon as possible. Be glad that he lets you know when he needs changing. He will soon learn that it is up to him to get relief from that discomfort. The same goes for his crying from hunger. But don't pick him up everytime he cries from hunger. This would not only train him to be continuously demanding, but would spoil him. Always honor his cry for essentials. Of course, use your adult judgment as to how much or how often he should eat.

Generally let the child suffer the consequences of his own misdeeds. This of course must be qualified by the need for his general safety. Don't let him fall off the house roof if he climbs up there, but when he crawls under the table and tries to stand up, let him bump his head. If he wants to touch something hot, let him do it if it is not hot enough to burn his skin or cause a blister. A child who is always shielded from every pain will not learn to take care of himself. If he carelessly or deliberately breaks his toy, don't replace it right away. If you are wise, you will let your child suffer loss which comes through his own misdeeds while he is small and the loss isn't so great. In this way you can teach him to be careful when he is older and the loss may be more serious!

Put your child into situations in which you show that you trust him. When it is reasonably safe, let your little girl carry some of the chinaware to the table when you set the table for a meal. Be prepared to take it in the right spirit if she drops it and it breaks. You will have trusted her, and if she fails, she will need your moral support rather than a reprimand. You might do well to let her carry another piece of china to help her regain confidence.

When my wife and I were taking care of some of our grandchildren, the three-year-old insisted on helping set the table. Grandma consented and gave her some plates and cups. She happily carried them to the dining room and placed them on the table although she had to get on a chair sometimes to put things in the right places. What a loss it would have been to her and to our enjoyment of the children if Grandma had said, "No, you might break the dishes."

This matter of trust works both ways. That is, you trust your child and he trusts you. Trust *must* be mutual for your child to benefit most.

When each of our four children was about two or three, we had a little game we would play together. I would lift the little one to some ledge or the top of a chest of drawers, and lower my body to be just below him. I then held my hands toward him and told him to jump, letting him know I would catch him. At first he was a bit afraid, but finally he trusted me and jumped. After I had caught him and he knew he could trust me, he wanted to do it some more.

I trusted him to trust me, and he trusted me to catch him. One weakness in this little game came about when I was not present. Esther stood on the banister of a fairly high porch and told a playmate to stand down on the ground and catch her when she jumped. The playmate tried to catch her, but being too heavy for her friend, Esther fell to the ground and hurt herself. By this she learned not to trust just anyone. This was valuable to her, but the physical hurt could easily have been more serious.

A young man in his higher teens had about three months free from school and wanted to do some voluntary work in India, helping the missionaries there. He got the consent of his parents and made his own travel arrangements to India. This was quite a venture since he knew none of the Indian languages. He arrived in India, and the difference in culture and climate made it very interesting and exciting to him. After he was there a few weeks, he wrote to his parents expressing his sincere thanks to them for trusting him to go alone. Their trusting him impressed him more as he saw the dangers and differences in that country.

Assign regular home chores to your child. He will be happier for having a share in the work. This, of course, must begin while he is quite small. It does not begin with merely giving the youngster something to do. It begins with your loving him and holding his confidence. If he loves you and believes in you, he will also appreciate his home. If he appreciates his home, he will be more willing to help in it. You don't win his love and confidence by being easy and permissive with him. The child who is held strictly to proper conduct is the child who feels secure. Assign regular tasks to him. Don't be reminding him every day to do his work. Keep your eye open so you know whether it is done or not.

A certain girl I knew—she was about eighteen—was hired as a maid in my cousin's house. She seemingly was not taught by her mother to see work to be done without being prompted each time. When she had finished one chore for her employer, she would stand and wait for further instructions. After a while my cousin, who was ill, would say to her, "Maggie, I think you should scrub the pantry floor." To which Maggie would reply, "I was just thinking about that." That was the formula for about every job she did, "I was just thinking about that." How much better it would have been if she had been taught to assume responsibility at home.

Occasionally assign a task to your child which is almost too difficult for him. At first when you do this, stay close by to give assistance, if it is needed. This will do several things. It will feed his ego, be a challenge for him, make him grow in his abilities, prove your confidence in him, and make him feel more responsible.

This is what God also is always doing for his children— giving us work beyond our abilities and then giving us strength and help to do that work.

Keep your child aware of the fact that the gifts God has given us are for use in good purposes. I have two hands that must work for Him, two feet for walking carefully, two eyes to keep clear, two ears to gain knowledge, time to use wisely, opportunities to use and abilities to exercise in good works. For all these gifts I must be thankful and consider myself responsible for what I do with them.

The child should be kept aware as he develops physically and mentally that God made him, is feeding him, and loves him so much that Jesus died on the cross. It is through this that we can really live right and live eternally with Him after this life. It is a serious matter for anyone to misuse his body, mind, or time since they all really belong to God.

If your child is to be trained in your home to be a responsible adult, he must be loved, trusted, taught, corrected, encouraged, guided, understood and watched by good parents.

I had gotten off the train at ten o'clock one stormy night during the hot season in India and set out on my homeward journey of fourteen miles. It was pitch dark as a cloud-cover had hidden the stars and there was a new moon. I stopped at a friend's house for a lantern to light my path, and he also gave me a box of matches in case the wind would blow out the flame.

I started out across the fields, but soon the strong wind blew out my light. Kneeling down beside a rice bank, I made a tent with my coat and re-lit the lantern. Before long the light went out again, and I didn't get very far before I had used all my matches. Then I stood all alone in the black night unable to see even a few feet ahead.

Stopping to think, I scanned the horizon for any possible lights I might see. Seeing one tiny light in the distance, I stumbled toward it, not knowing whether I would be headed toward home or not. I had lost all sense of direction and desperately wanted to get in somewhere. Rice banks and pitch darkness hindered my progress, but I stumbled along and finally arrived in the village to which the light had guided me. There I found a mud house with a lantern hanging from the roof of the porch—the only light that could be seen in the village.

The man sitting on the porch wondered where I was going so late at night in a storm such as this. Upon hearing my intentions, he replied, "No, I won't let you go on tonight. You cannot make it. I will give you a bed, and in the morning you can go home." I accepted his kind invitation. In the morning I awoke refreshed and found that the storm had subsided. He insisted that I eat a delicious breakfast of fried eggs, small cakes, and a cup of tea.

Before leaving, I asked him why he had hung his lantern on the porch, and he said, "I just thought someone might be lost and by this he could find his way." I prayed for him and for me before leaving, thankful to God for His love and to my Mohammedan friend for his hospitality.

23

Hospitality

Hospitality is near the top of the list of Christian virtues. It is one of the marks of a true Christian, although many non-Christians are also very hospitable.

Hospitality can be taught as proper conduct, but the true hospitality of which I speak is more than a formal part of social behavior. Its highest form stems from the attitude of wanting to help others in need because of the love of God in the heart.

The baby's first lesson in hospitality comes from his mother's tender care and concern for his welfare and happiness. If a person would never experience kindness or hospitality from someone, he would also not be able to show it to others.

There is hardly a child who has not had kindness shown to him sometime. Normally, his mother fed him and cared for him when he was young. But what I am discussing is not just the ordinary care for an infant, but the extra love that human parents are capable of showing. It is this extra affection and concern that counts. If you care for your child only because you are expected to feed him and keep him clean, then he may never know how to be kind to those who are not his direct responsibility.

The tone of your voice, the expression on your face, and the kindness of your touch all affect your child. You will be well repaid for any extra time you spend with him to give him that extra affection. This is one reason why I do not favor having baby-sitters unless it is a real necessity. I still have some idea of how it felt to have my head lying on my mother's arm, and seeing her smiling face as she looked at me.

The second step in training your child in hospitality is your example. This tells much more than your words of exhortation. Remember it is for a good purpose that your children come running to you when you go to the door to answer a knock. They do it out of curiosity. They want to see who is there, but underneath that, the real purpose is learning. If they are properly trained, they will stand back a little and silently watch and listen. They will agree that what you do and say to the stranger is right. Any sensible Christian mother will never send her child to answer the knock by saying, "Mother isn't here." And when you have visitors in your home, don't send the children to the playroom. Let them be right with you, properly behaved, unless you don't want them to see how you treat your company. Parents who are truly hospitable will have children who will be like them.

Sincerity in hospitality is a must. I don't know of any way to teach a child to be sincere in his kindness to others if you as parents are not sincere in your hospitality. If your children hear you talking unkindly about your guests after they are gone, they will remember how nice you were to them while they were visiting with you.

Maybe you say, "I'm always careful not to talk unkindly about others in our children's hearing." That still does not make you sincere. If you have any adverse feelings toward others, you must make it right in the proper way. You must not harbor such feelings in your heart. You can't hide them just by not voicing them in front of your children.

Your child will sense your love for people if it is genuine. This they will learn best by your example. It is hard or impossible to treat people with genuine hospitality if you would just as soon not have them around. If there is a lack of general love for people, you must do something

176

about it. This is essential as a part of hospitality. Hospitality is really love for others being exercised.

If your child brings one or more friends along home, don't reprimand him or discourage him from doing it again. Instead, be kind to him and his friends, helping him to be hospitable. However, if he overdoes this and brings so many friends home that it disrupts your home life, you can correct it tactfully.

Love for people does not mean tolerating all the evil found in them. One long-haired young man asked me what I thought of long hair. I frankly told him that I don't like long hair and disapprove of it, but I love the person behind that long hair and try hard not to let it hinder my love for him. He appreciated my expression.

"Be not forgetful to entertain strangers." This is a command given in the New Testament. We are not to be hospitable only to friends and relatives in our own circle, but also to strangers! It is a benefit to the family and to the stranger to be concerned for those who are not of our own family. It also is a necessary part of obedience to the New Testament doctrine of evangelism.

Once a "road-walker" or, as we sometimes say, a "tramp," knocked on a minister's door and asked for something to eat. The minister, who had four or five young children, let the man into the house. It was mealtime and they invited him to eat with them at the table. This was a very wise thing for the minister to do, for it was a good experience for the children. Through this experience they learned a number of valuable lessons.

When other children come to your house to play, you can do one of two things about it. You can either dismiss the children from your concern and go about your work letting the children play as they will, or you can curtail your own work while the young visitors are in the house, partly supervising their activities. The latter of these two options is by far the better.

Your children might be better trained than the visitors, or the visitors might be better trained than yours in matters of play and sharing. In either case, it is an opportunity for your family to benefit by the experience. It is almost certain that among young children little clashes or frictions will come up and they will need help.

Great care must be taken in such a situation. You might without intention, show a favor to one of the visitors and not show the same favor to your own child. This would create a problem in the relation between you and your child. I remember sixty-five years ago when I thought my father was partial in favoring my visitor. Children will notice this and feel it. I was at fault for I should have been glad to have my visitor favored, but as a child I did not understand all this.

Teach your children to favor the visitor themselves by giving them their toys to use while they are in your home.

The most inhospitable thing you can do is gossip about the neighbors. When doing this, the neighbors are not present to defend themselves. For your own sake and for your children's sakes, say only good things about your neighbors when they are absent and treat them to true hospitality when they are with you. Make it a point to never gossip even when the children are small, and when they are old enough that they gossip, you should strictly forbid it. This will be a priceless heritage to your children.

A noted lecturer had an appointment to speak to a very important assembly. He was ready to start from home early enough to be present on time. The one who had promised to take him to the meeting came much too late. It was carelessness on the driver's part that caused him to be twenty minutes late for his appointment. When he arose to speak, he simply said, "I am sorry to be late," and proceeded with his lecture.

It was not his fault that he was late. Many a person would have taken the opportunity to make his defense and thus support his own pride, but this humble man did not do that.

Many are the times when the humble person must "swallow" the mistakes of others, but the Bible tells us that pride is followed by destruction and a fall follows a haughty spirit. On the other hand, it also says that the meek are happy.

24

Humility

Humility can be a virtue, even in a child, but it is the kind of virtue that ceases to be when it is acknowledged. Satan is very subtle. His first sin was pride, and if he can get a person to be proud of his humility, he is pleased.

We are born with a perverted nature. Pride is present from infancy and will soon show up in a young child. He will be defensive, or assertive, to the point where he will tell a lie to defend himself. The child is innocent when he first does this because it is by his natural instinct that he does it, and his moral sense is not yet developed.

When your child is young, the nature of his pride or humility will pretty much run parallel with yours. If you have a false pride or false humility, he will also. One young girl often got into trouble with the neighbor children. When her mother heard about it, the girl would deny what the neighbors said about her. Promptly her mother would call the mothers of the other children and insist that their accusations against her daughter were not true. She declared that her girl said she didn't do those things and added, "I know my girl doesn't lie." She was too proud to admit that her girl did tell lies. And when the girl heard her mother talking to the neighbors this way, she became more defensive, untruthful, and proud. It became a vicious process which worsened the situation. The reason was not so much that the girl lied as it was that the mother wouldn't admit that she could be lying.

What this mother should have done was to apologize to the neighbors in the girl's hearing. She should have told her

181

daughter that several neighbors complaining about the same thing would not likely be wrong, and we must remember that we could be wrong. She should have urged her to go back to play with the children and be nice to them.

It would have been very damaging to the girl, however, for the mother to "explode" and sharply reprimand the daughter for telling a lie. As it was, she damaged the girl's spirit by taking her part and defending her. What she did was probably more damaging to the girl than the other would have been.

The mother should not make too much of a small child's lying. What caused him to lie is worse and should be of more concern to a mother. You as a parent should never express surprise at your child's misconduct. If you express surprise and sharply rebuke the child, you only undermine his confidence in you. Defending him, however, will bring the same results.

You must always remember that being proud, untruthful, or mean to others is the natural thing for your child. Keep a long-range view on the matter and work tactfully to correct his conduct. You could tell him, "I know you did wrong and lied about it, but I love you and I want to help you do better." In some natural way, show your affection. Love must always rule. When he is a little older and it is obvious he purposely did wrong, then severe punishment would be required.

Breaking a child's spirit does not make him humble. It may make him a vandal or make him antisocial. You must avoid breaking a child's spirit.

Danny grew up in a very abnormal home. His parents had been separated and reunited various times. His father often beat him severely. His mother would continuously shout and rarely say anything to him in a kind voice. When I went to visit the family, the mother would tell me all of his capers and misconduct in his presence. Sometimes when Danny was roughly spoken to or treated meanly, he would

182

take off his shoe and throw it through the window shattering the glass. One time his mother told me Danny had thrown his shoe through the glass door of the china cupboard. Danny was present when she told me. My heart went out in sympathy for the poor boy. Whenever I visited in that home, Danny would voluntarily walk over to me and place his arm around my neck. He did this up to the time he was ten years of age. The poor boy was neither proud nor humble. He was broken.

Self-debasement is not humility. It is a type of spirit-suicide in which the person breaks his own spirit.

If you continually nag or blame your child and never praise him, he may begin to believe that what you are accusing him of is true, and the results are a very destructive kind of self-debasement.

Sometimes the continual nagging of a child will result in his becoming rebellious or criminal-like instead of self-debasing. Self-debasement may be a severe form of extreme humiliation but not true humility, while rebellion is a dangerous form of extreme pride. True humility comes only through the new birth when one becomes a whole person in Christ Jesus. When one sees himself as God sees him, he will be truly humble.

You must help the child to know himself. This is a most difficult thing for even a grown person to achieve. When it comes to judging ourselves, we are hampered with strong prejudices and biases. It is easier to judge another person whom we don't love as much.

If your little boy wants to push the lawn mower, let him try. He may not move it an inch, but it looked so easy when you did it. Now he has learned something about himself that he never knew before.

Sometimes I ask a very young child, "Are you a good boy?" His answer is always, "Yes," When I ask a boy of six, he will say, "Not always." The older boy has learned to know himself.

Our granddaughter will say about one o'clock in the afternoon, "I am sleepy." She doesn't object to taking her nap. She knows something about herself.

An infant is continually learning to know more about himself. At first he doesn't know he has hands, but when he discovers it, he reaches for everything. He learns that when his eyes are covered he can't see. He discovers it is with his eyes that he sees. When he is older, he needs to know more about himself if he is to do his best. It pleases him when he learns he can make the room light up by flipping the switch. The mother tries to get her little girl to sing, and when she discovers she can sing, she sings most of the time.

Years ago, a little girl who was more than two years old didn't walk yet. This caused her parents great concern. She always liked to play with her father's detachable cuffs. One morning the little girl was playing on the floor at one end of the dining room and her father was hurrying to go to work. As he came through the dining room he laid his cuffs on the dining table. The little girl saw them and suddenly jumped up and ran over to the table and got the cuffs. She surprised herself and her parents, for she hadn't realized she could walk.

When the child is about twelve, he should be led by his parents to know that he has trouble being good. When he discovers that something in him always makes him want to do the wrong thing, he can be led to look for outside help which he can get by giving his life to Christ.

You must help your child to be a good loser. Some young people insist that they can do anything they try. Some can indeed do more than others, but it is good for them to have their pride trimmed down sometimes.

If your third-grader comes home crying because he failed in his test and you know he honestly tried hard, let him know that it is only natural to fail sometimes. Encourage him to try again. He might be better fitted to try harder by having failed once.

If someone in school stole your child's pencil, help him realize that happiness doesn't depend on having a particular pencil. There are other things in life worth more than the best pencil. The ability not to cry over his loss is worth more than the best pencil in the world. It may be unholy pride that makes him cry over the loss or makes him fight to get it back.

You can't teach your child humility. You *can* teach a child not to think of himself more highly than he ought to think, as the Bible tells us. You can teach him balanced self-evaluation, and to love his neighbor as himself. Everyone must love himself properly if he is to love his neighbor as he should. But if he loves himself more than he loves others, he will no longer be humble.

A young child just naturally loves himself, but he is likely humble. He will also love others, especially when they love him. It is after his playmate takes away his toy that his self-love rises in protest and his natural pride asserts itself. If Mother tells him to let his playmate have his toy for a while because he would also like to play with it, he will likely calm down and even begin to love the other child more. You didn't teach him to be humble, but he is more humble because you helped him break his pride.

You know that the Bible teaches us to return good for evil. This is the best therapy existing, and for both parties. If someone does me evil, his pride is up and mine is provoked also. If I return good to him, it helps both of us since it breaks our pride.

When your child becomes old enough to understand right and wrong and discovers he cannot cope with all his evil tendencies, he will need to turn to the only sure help for the human heart—to be regenerated by the power of the risen Christ.

The humble person is always stable and strong in adversity. The proud person cannot overcome his enemy because he stumbles over his entanglements with self.

A minister I knew well became involved in an indiscretion. One day I heard another minister talk about the first one, severely condemning him. This second minister gave the impression that he would never commit such an evil. He revealed his own pride. Some time later he fell in committing adultery. His fall was worse than the first minister's. A third man, a layman, came to the first minister and tried to console him for he was very much broken in contrition. This layman was very humble and acknowledged that anyone might be overtaken in such a fault. He prayed for the penitent preacher and for himself. He was a great help to him, and he never fell into grievous sin himself.

The humble person is always the most trustworthy. Strive to help your child to a balanced humility. If you praise him for something in which he did well, don't compare him with others, saying, "You did better than Tommy did." If you need to correct him, don't tell him, "Other people are doing better than you." In the first situation you may foster improper pride in him. In the second, you may break his spirit.

Always lead your child to improve on himself rather than to try to be better than some others. The Bible tells us that when we compare ourselves among ourselves we are not wise. II Cor. 10:12. It doesn't take teen-agers long to label one who thinks himself above the others. Young people will also be disrespectful to anyone in the group who has an inferiority complex.

One who is well balanced in his humility is the most useful to his group, and also in the Lord's service.

Thirty-five pupils in grades one to eight and one teacher comprised a certain one-room country school. One boy about ten years old was a problem, and because of him the school was considered a very difficult one. The school board had hired a mature man to teach the school, thinking he could handle the situation. Before long he had to whip the boy, but the whipping didn't help, and the reaction to the whipping led to the teacher's resignation. The board hired another man with a good reputation, and the same thing happened. The board met again, and one of the men recommended a certain young lady who he thought could handle the school even though she was small in stature. He had a hard time convincing the rest of the board members, but they finally agreed.

Soon after the new teacher came, the boy, seated about half-way back in the school room, misbehaved again. The teacher remained seated in the front of the room and asked Johnny to come to her. He shook his head, and with a mischievous grin, he said, "No." She calmly urged him in very kind tones to come. "I won't hurt you," she said. After some time he slowly moved out of his seat and walked to the teacher's chair. She gently pulled him on to her lap and put her arm around him. Then she looked down at his face and said, "Johnny, I do love you. You don't want to be bad, do you?" Johnny shook his head and finally said, "No, I don't want to be bad." By now he had tears in his eyes. She talked a little more with him and sent him to his seat. The boy never made any more trouble for her, and she won the respect of the whole school. She finished the term successfully.

Why did she succeed? She first loved him, and this caused him to love her. That was the process that won the day.

25

Love

Parents, if your child learns to love from your example, then you will have given him his most valuable asset for most any situation he might face in his life.

Parents must never be afraid of their child. The Bible tells us that perfect love casts out fear. Love and fear simply do not live together, for where true love is there is also mutual trust. This, of course, refers to relationships between two or more persons. However, a person may have love in his heart for one person, but fear for another.

Occasionally I see parents who are afraid of their children. They fear to disagree with them, to correct them, or even to live with them. This makes for an impossible situation. The most natural human relationship in which to find love is a family of parents and children. And when it is lost there, the tragedy is all the greater.

Your love for your child must be strong enough that you would give your life for him. Love begets love. If you have this kind of love for your child, it will make it easier for your child to love you. I have heard of parents who have sent their child out of the house because he had done something disgraceful. Our love for our children should be strong enough that it wouldn't let go even if the child would become a criminal.

Love sometimes carries a stick. Adherence to rules and strict discipline is a part of true love. When a parent says, "I love my child too much to punish him," he reveals a sadly mistaken concept of love. That would be like saying, "I love my child too much to keep him from going wrong."

This would be a contradiction. If you love your child enough, you will do all you can to keep him from going wrong.

Regardless of modern teachings in child training or psychology, corporal punishment must still be applied at times. No doubt, most hippies that travel across the continents today would not be on the road if they had been brought up strictly—even with corporal punishment at times—while they were young children.

Real love comes from God. We don't learn to love by attending classes on love nor from reading about it in books. Man is created in the image of God and human love is instinctive. But it must be developed and cultivated. The best way to train your child to love is to love him. He will catch it from you.

On the other hand, that love can be destroyed. Harboring suspicion can do it. The longer you continue to suspect your loved one, the weaker your love will become. It may finally die. A parent who continually suspects his child of wrong, presents an ugly picture and destroys love.

Failure to nurture or feed love in your loved one brings on loss of love. Mere neglect will finally cause love to die. There are many ways to feed the love in your child. For a young child, the physical expression of love to him is a must. The child that is not cuddled by his parents is being deprived of a necessary element in his emotional development. Remember, there is a difference between cuddling and coddling. Coddling is harmful, but cuddling is not.

Rejection will also destroy love. The unwed teen-ager loved her parents, but when she became pregnant, they disowned her just at the time when she most needed their love. What a tragedy!

The young son who comes home crying because he has done something wrong and his schoolmates all turned against him needs love. The mother who simply says, "Why didn't you behave?" and then pays no more attention to him when he needs a reassuring hug and kiss from her, injures the boy's love for her and may crush his spirit.

Real love is divine love. It is higher than human love. It is shed abroad in the hearts of Christians by the Holy Spirit. Of course, you remember, you are your child's first god. Don't let your love break down. If you have the love of God in your heart, you will love your child in all circumstances.

The love of God will hold on when other love would fail. Jesus tells us to love our enemies. That is not natural. This requires divine love within us. That love cannot be killed, although it can be thwarted. It can be turned down, rejected. But it will continue to love just the same.

The love of God comes only by a miracle of grace. You, dear parent, must be born again. Otherwise the love of God cannot come to you and transform your life. When you receive the Holy Spirit, you will receive the love of God. This is stronger than any human love.

Furthermore, if you yourself are not born again, you are not fully fitted to train your child. Before you can properly train your child according to God's will, you must experience the transforming power of God in your own life and submit yourself to the Lordship of Jesus Christ. Then you can also lead your child into that most glorious of all experiences. Only then can his proper training be assured.